Incarceration and Health Care

Arts, Creativities, and Learning Environments in Global Perspectives

Series Editors

Tatiana Chemi (*Aalborg University*)
Anu M. Mitra (*Union Institute & University*)

VOLUME 12

The titles published in this series are listed at *brill.com/acle*

Incarceration and Health Care

A Visual Journey through the Lens of Activist Art

By

Tamara White

BRILL

LEIDEN | BOSTON

Cover illustration: Image by Tamara White

All chapters in this book have undergone peer review.

The Library of Congress Cataloging-in-Publication Data is available online at https://catalog.loc.gov

Typeface for the Latin, Greek, and Cyrillic scripts: "Brill". See and download: brill.com/brill-typeface.

ISSN 2589-9813
ISBN 978-90-04-71059-7 (paperback)
ISBN 978-90-04-71060-3 (hardback)
ISBN 978-90-04-71061-0 (e-book)
DOI 10.1163/9789004710610

To those who have faced the inconceivable and emerged with resilience and redemption, this book is dedicated to your inspiring journey of transformation

••
•

Contents

Acknowledgements

The intersection of healthcare management and incarceration originated from my interest in focusing on diabetes in my dissertation research. I would not be writing about this topic if not for my daughter, Electra. Thank you for being an example of strength and grace. I am in awe. Thank you to Alex and Lucy for your constant enthusiasm, encouragement, and levity when I needed it most. I love all of you more than the moon, stars, and the sky. Nothing I do in this world equals having all of you in my life. I would also like to credit Dr. Saleh Adi for his guidance as an imperturbable and caring provider who inspires those living with diabetes while promoting a life beyond the confines of A1C levels.

This book would not be possible without the encouragement of Dr. Anu Mitra, who has been my guiding light throughout my doctoral program and the stages of this endeavor. My museum posse – Kathryn Turley-Sonne, Bruce Maggi, and AC Panella, who have sustained me over the past several years and are now contributors to the birth of Bader + Simon. Paula, for setting an example of what is possible when you push through. To my cheerleader and the Louise, to my Thelma, Carolyn Jones, for her walking pep talks and constant belief in me. To Mina and Adam for their continual encouragement, and to my "G.M." for their creativity, inspiration, and friendship.

A special thank you to Dr. Brie Williams and Dr. Rob Kahn for their insightful work in bringing inclusion, equity, support, and solutions to vulnerable communities that are frequently overlooked. Peter Margolis and Gwenn Lennox provided many introductions that contributed to my research. Additionally, I would like to thank the many specialists and formerly incarcerated individuals who requested anonymity. Your stories offer insight and exemplify the fortitude required when living and working within the carceral system.

I am immensely grateful to the artists who provided me with permission to include their work within these pages: Appleton, Shanequa Benitez, Sara Bennett, Russell Craig, Kathryn DeMarco, Guerilla Girls, Joy Hoop, James Yaya Hough, Jesse Krimes, Steven and William Ladd, Jared Owens, Diego Rios, Sable Elyse Smith, Daniel Sundahl, Zeph Vondenhuevel, Kenneth Webb, and Aimee Wissman. The visual narrative of your art surpasses the boundaries and capabilities of words, providing a point of view on the actualities of incarceration and managing chronic health conditions.

Dr. Bidhan Roy was instrumental in providing information about and access to witness the inner workings of the prison system. Through his work with Words Uncaged, Dr. Roy leads released citizens into the next phase of their lives with introspection, education, and hope. Numerous other individuals, too many to name, have offered me friendship, advice, information, and encouragement along the way. Please forgive me, for the sake of brevity, for not listing everyone, yet know I am forever grateful. Including my extended family, who likely view me with a strange curiosity yet are always optimistic about my endeavors.

Margaret Meade correctly stated, "Never doubt that a small group of thoughtful, committed individuals can change the world. In fact, it's the only thing that ever has." It is this small group of people to whom I am forever beholden, and I trust that together, collectively, change will come.

She believed she could, and so she did.

Figures

Introduction

Of all the forms of inequality, injustice in health care is the most
shocking and inhumane.

MARTIN LUTHER KING, JR.

∴

Prior to the days of desperately searching for my dissertation topic, I had not
readily considered the overlap of healthcare management and incarceration.
I did not fully appreciate the immediacy with which art can tacitly convey
vital information. Focusing on design thinking and museum studies, I visited
museums and galleries during my wanderings and experienced the range of
exhibition possibilities. However, it was when I walked through the doors of
the Legacy Museum in Montgomery, Alabama, that I understood how power-
fully and effectively a compelling exhibit and installation could communicate
critical information. As one of the last in my museum studies cohort to finalize
my dissertation topic, I was desperately searching, and the harder I tried, the
more my brain seized up. On a road trip to the Equal Justice Initiative's space,
I finally found what I was searching for.

Founded in 1989 by Bryan Stevenson, attorney and best-selling author of
Just Mercy, the Equal Justice Initiative (EJI) provides legal representation to
those who have been "illegally convicted, unfairly sentenced, or abused in state
jails or prisons" (EJI, 2018). Furthermore, the organization challenges death
penalty cases, assists newly released individuals in acclimating to society, and
provides support with necessities such as obtaining a driver's license, housing,
and employment. A significant focus of EJI's work is overturning or reducing
sentences for children tried as adults, wrongful convictions, and prison conditions. EJI believes that "ending mass incarceration is the civil rights issue of
our time" (EJI, 2018).

The Legacy Museum highlights the transition from slavery to mass incarceration. Located on the site of a former warehouse in Montgomery where
enslaved people were forced into harsh labor conditions, the museum is now in
its second home with space to exhibit and encapsulate the horror and history
of slavery. In addition to the Legacy Museum, the non-profit organization runs
The National Memorial for Peace and Justice, a memorial dedicated to the

legacy of enslaved Black Americans terrorized by lynching, racial segregation, and the burden of presumed guilt and police violence.

I had arrived at the Legacy Museum weary after having already visited the Smithsonian National Museum of African American History and Culture in Washington, D.C. It was 2019, and I was on a cross-country trip trying to narrow down the focus of my dissertation topic. With over 40,000 artifacts that tell the story of African American life, history, and culture scattered amongst four floors, the D.C. museum provides visitors with the sobering facts of the slave trade and the trauma and turmoil that followed. The experience left me feeling emotionally raw and questioning the injustice that feels so ubiquitous in our divisive world.

The Legacy Museum's immersive exhibitions included audio of incarcerated children telling their stories overhead. Mock visiting booths presenting holographic characters that describe the circumstances of their journey; a documentary looped in a dimly lit room explained the torturous conditions at Angola Prison in Louisiana. This last experience sent me rushing to a bathroom stall, feeling nauseous and hollow. It was as if my body could no longer contain the anguish and torment building inside me. All I could do was sit and cry, trying to exorcise the helplessness and anger the video elicited.

While I did not grow up with privilege, I have the advantage of living in a world that supports my skin color. Visiting both museums made me hyperaware of my ability to move within the world with relative ease without questioning authority figures' motives or operating with guarded skepticism. Similarly, I can afford basic needs and necessary medical supplies for my family, specifically for my middle child, who was diagnosed with type 1 diabetes just before her tenth birthday. Having a child with diabetes and understanding the precariousness of managing an unpredictable disease, I suddenly thought, "What does someone with diabetes do while incarcerated?" while standing amid Bryan Stevenson's visual brainchild. The effectiveness of the Legacy Museum space revealed a perspective I may not have otherwise discovered.

The exhibits within the space were overwhelming with an amalgamation of sounds, visual images of enslaved people, interactive holograms that mimic visiting room spaces, and letters on the walls from children who had been tried and convicted as adults. The curated exhibition exemplifies the power of art in saying what words sometimes cannot. This experience reminded me of the powerlessness that occurs when dealing with a chronic illness such as diabetes. I remembered what I experienced upon hearing of my daughter's diagnosis. I empathize with the lack of control and fear that would occur for someone trying to manage diabetes while incarcerated.

My daughter had been sick for days. We assumed she had a virus, filling her with liquids, Gatorade, and 7-up and keeping her home from school. Like slow-moving molasses, I watched my daughter shrink in size. We later discovered that her weight dropped from 62 to 42 pounds in one week. The impetus to seek emergency care arrived abruptly one morning when my daughter, sleeping beside me, awakened at 6 a.m., vomiting water. Without pause, I grabbed a pillow and blanket and put her in the backseat of my car, driving not to the nearest children's hospital but to the emergency room where I knew we'd be seen immediately. The receptionist took one look at my daughter and swiftly put us in a room.

There are moments in life that slow to a rolling stop like script notes movie directors add for effect. This was one of them. With my daughter lying so small in an adult-sized hospital bed, the doctor caringly put her hand on my daughter's leg, looked her in the eye, and said, "Electra, you have diabetes." The words didn't quite register as my brain tried to make sense of the diagnosis. "What? What does that mean?" Later, after the doctor had left the room and the nurse had finally found a vein that would receive an IV, my beautiful child looked at me and weakly said, "All I want for my birthday is not to have diabetes." I thought I would vomit from the guttural turmoil of being unable to make this happen for her.

The circumstance with my daughter brought forth a previously obscure awareness. My naive understanding of diabetes was an inability to eat sugar. From that first day of her diagnosis, I confidently told my daughter, "If you can't eat sugar, none of us will eat sugar. We're in this together." before learning that people with diabetes can have sugar as long as it's balanced with insulin, before comprehending how the body breaks down carbohydrates into sugar, which provides energy to cells, before understanding how for many, the pancreas releases insulin. For my daughter and the millions with Type 1 diabetes, however, insulin must be injected intravenously through a syringe or insulin pump.

My understanding of what is required for consistent and adequate health outcomes when living with diabetes is a core reason why the EJI Legacy Museum impacted me. The daily requirements of diabetes management elicit images of an internal prison, never having a day off. For those living behind prison walls, it's as if they have received a double sentence to contend with while having little control over either situation. My daughter's diagnosis has brought consciousness and empathy for those burdened by health conditions and the need for constant care.

Waiting for prescription refills at the Children's Hospital pharmacy, I became acutely aware of the compromised decision-making families experience when they have a child with a chronic illness. I was grateful that the eighty-dollar co-pay our insurance required was an easy lift for us. Nevertheless, as I looked around the Oakland facility, I suspected it was not as manageable for others. Without health insurance, insulin can cost upward of $400 per vile, and most individuals require two vials per month. However, an $80 co-pay can tip the scales toward scarcity when living paycheck to paycheck. How, as a society, can we ask parents to choose between food and life-saving medications? We are sentencing parents to an impossible either-or scenario with unimaginable outcomes regardless of their choice. How can we pose that question to anyone? Between choosing necessary supplies to keep themselves or their child alive rather than paying for necessities?

I understand that managing a chronic health condition is complicated under the best circumstances. After walking through the Legacy Museum and its vast sensory-laden exhibits, I felt unsettled as I questioned the challenge and complexity of living behind bars with a dangerous ailment, especially a chronic one that requires constant, immediate attention. Trying to manage a chronic health condition when someone else controls the essential supplies and medications is an additional form of imprisonment- one which my daughter was fortunate to escape but which is not equitable for others.

Research has shown that incarcerated people have a higher rate of infectious disease and chronic health issues than their non-incarcerated counterparts. Forty percent of incarcerated survey respondents described themselves as having at least one chronic medical condition (Maruschak et al., 2015). A 2009 report found a higher-than-average rate of hypertension, arthritis, cervical cancer, and hepatitis for incarcerated populations (Binswanger et al., 2009, as cited in Crane & Pascoe, 2020). The most immediate threat for incarcerated people has traditionally been physical violence. The COVID pandemic of 2020 revealed a similar threat- the extreme vulnerability of those behind bars when COVID clusters infiltrated jails and prisons within the United States.

Understanding the precariousness of healthcare management behind bars, the Equal Justice Initiative opened up EJI Health in June 2023, a clinic whose mission is to provide healthcare services to those recently released from correctional facilities and other vulnerable populations in Alabama. After spending thirty years providing legal assistance to Alabama communities in need, EJI is now focusing on further expanding its services to confront poverty by assisting the uninsured and those needing crucial health care. Stevenson stated that "EJI Health can make a positive contribution to helping people re-enter society but also promote healthier communities and improved public safety" (EJI, 2023).

We are not all born on an equal playing field, and those behind bars face additional disadvantages. The formerly incarcerated artist Jesse Krimes aptly points out, "We're all offenders" (LaRocca, 2018, para. 2). We have all likely done something to break the law; some have been fortunate to escape punishment. Ultimately, we are all human. There is immense humanity in providing adequate healthcare to every individual, regardless of their place in our world.

My journey through the Legacy Museum showed me the incredible capacity of visual storytelling. Of the ways in which art can serve as an avenue for change and activism, oftentimes expressing emotions that words alone cannot. I hope this book can shed light on the extreme health compromises for incarcerated people and that the included artwork can shift your perspective not only of health care and incarceration but also of the immense power of art as activism to inform, educate, and agitate for societal changes.

References

Crane, J. T., & Pascoe, K. (2021). Becoming institutionalized: Incarceration as a chronic health condition. *Medical Anthropology Quarterly, 35*(3), 307–326. https://doi.org/ 10.1111/maq.12621

Equal Justice Initiative. (2018, December 11). *Half of Americans have family members who have been incarcerated.* https://eji.org/news/half-of-americans-have-family- members-who-have-been-incarcerated/

Equal Justice Initiative. (2023, June 5). *EJI opens new clinic providing health services to vulnerable communities.* https://eji.org/news/eji-opens-new-clinic-providing- health-services-to-vulnerable-communities/

LaRocca, L. (2018, February 7). Art activist Jesse Krimes brings awareness to mass incarceration. *Baltimore Magazine.* https://www.baltimoremagazine.com/section/ artsentertainment/art-activist-jesse-krimes-brings-awareness-mass-incarceration/

Maruschak, L. M., Berzofsky, M., & Unangst, J. (2016, October 4). *Medical problems of state and federal prisoners and jail inmates, 2011–12. U.S. Department of Justice. Bureau of Justice Statistics.* https://bjs.ojp.gov/content/pub/pdf/mpsfpji1112.pdf

CHAPTER 1

Social Determinants of Health

Disease only treats humans equally when our social orders treat humans equally.
JOHN GREEN

∴

The injustice I witnessed picking up my daughter's prescription at the pharmacy epitomizes how social determinants impact an individual's quality of health – factors contributing to health outcomes and an overall sense of well-being. The Centers for Disease Control and Prevention define *social determinants of health* as the conditions where people live, learn, work, and play and how those elements affect health and quality-of-life risks and outcomes. Five key areas fall under the determinants of health: healthcare access and quality, education access and quality, social and community context, economic stability, and neighborhood and built environment. Addressing these issues is essential to improve the health of those affected and reduce the historic and longstanding disparities that continue to exist. Reflecting on my experience at the Equal Justice Initiative's Museum spaces, I considered how profoundly a combination of hard evidence and visual representation can communicate critical information about these issues, including knowledge about incarcerated communities.

ReThink Health at The Ripple Foundation found that incarceration has a profound impact on health, as outlined in the reinforcing loop system

> Loop 1 – incarceration can create lifelong problems due to limited opportunities and exposure to "trauma, disease, chronic stress, social stigma, and exclusion" (Becker & Alexander, 2016, p. 2). It is very complicated to get out of this loop.
> Loop 2 – health impacts affect the children of incarcerated parents.
> Loop 3 – higher rates of incarceration have an impact on community health.

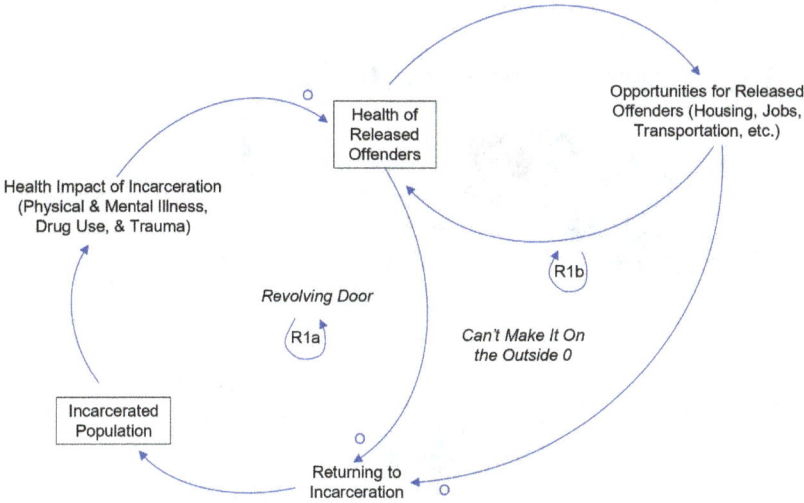

FIGURE 1   Loop system of incarceration (Source: Illustration of the reinforcing loop system
portraying the health impact of incarceration, Becker and Alexander. ReThink
Health at The Ripple Foundation. https://www.rethinkhealth.org/wp-content/
uploads/2016/04/ReThink-Health-March-17-Report-1.pdf)

Research has revealed that health conditions both arise and worsen due to
incarceration. The Department of Health and Human Services' Healthy People
2030 campaign has identified incarceration as a social determinant of health,
yet in order to improve the conditions for those impacted by the carceral system, an accurate data collecting and tracking system needs to be in place. This
circumstance is a challenging and frenetic task given the thousands of state
and local jurisdictions that operate in silos with very little communication on
a national level (Peterson & Brinkley-Rubenstein, 2021).

The concepts behind the term "social determinants of health" have been
in place for decades, first appearing in a 1967 Whitehall Study in the U.K. that
showed higher socioeconomic status reflected better health. In contrast, a
lower socioeconomic status demonstrated poorer health (Osmick & Wilson,
2020). The Whitehall Study revealed a consistent slant between poor and
wealthy populations (Wilkinson & Marmot, 2003). In 1985, Margaret Heckler,
Secretary of The U.S. Department of Health and Human Services, created a
task force on health conditions for Black and Minority citizens. The findings
confirmed that there was a disparity in the deaths and illnesses experienced
by Blacks and other minority groups. Hecker found the study results to be an
affront to the advancements in American medicine (Osmick & Wilson, 2020).

In 1999, epidemiologists Michael Marmot and Richard Wilkinson wrote the
book "Social Determinants of Health," highlighting the areas in which social

Social Determinants of Health

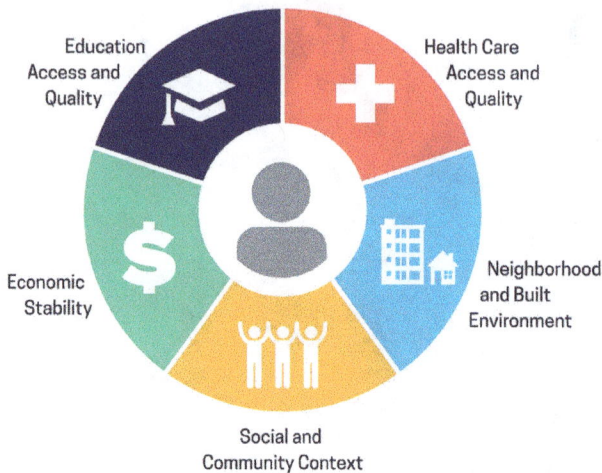

FIGURE 2   Social determinants of health (Source: Healthy People 2030, U.S. Department
of Health and Human Services, Office of Disease Prevention and Health Promotion.
https://health.gov/healthypeople/objectives-and-data/social-determinants-health)

circumstances impact one's quality of health. In their book, the researchers present information showing that few human aspects are unaffected by social determinants. Quality health is not simply about individual behavior or risk exposure but how the socially and economically structured way of life shapes and influences the health outcomes of a population.

People with scarce financial means have shorter life expectancies (Avendano & Kawachi, 2014). Limited options and resources can compromise health and put individuals in a precarious situation. With a lack of material goods, there is stress from "being poor, unemployed, socially excluded, or otherwise stigmatized," which includes the incarcerated population (Wilkinson & Marmot, 2003, p. 9). From our earliest beginnings, we need food, shelter, and a social network to feel valued and appreciated. Without these necessities, there is an increased risk of depression, drug usage, anxiety, and hopelessness, all traits that have an acute impact on physical and emotional health.

The correlation between socio-economic class and quality of health is significant to life expectancy. Individuals who are farther down the ladder "usually run at least twice the risk of serious illness and premature death as those near the top" (Wilkinson & Marmot, 2003, p. 10). Social determinants of health tend to impact the same group repeatedly, with circumstances accumulating over their lifetime. "The longer people live in stressful economic and social circumstances, the greater the psychological wear and tear they suffer, and the less likely they are to enjoy healthy old age" (Wilkinson & Marmot, 2003, p. 10).

I consider myself fortunate to have a housecleaner who tends to my home each week, whom I admire, trust, and have known for many years. Aware of my daughter's diabetes diagnosis she asked if it were possible to get less expensive insulin. I learned that her friend, living with diabetes and without health insurance, was paying out of pocket for insulin on her salary from working at a food stand. This individual was rationing her insulin supply, living in constant fear of going without necessary medical supplies or paying rent to avoid living on the street.

Since learning about this person's desperate situation, my daughter now passes along any remaining insulin she has on hand that has recently expired yet is still effective. Despite the prosperity of the United States, millions still need necessary health supplies. As the saying goes, it takes a village, and the volunteer-based organization Mutual Aid Diabetes exemplifies this by connecting those in need with those who can help. Formed in response to the growing insulin crisis in the United States, this group of people with diabetes created a hub to connect community members who need medication, insulin, supplies, and healthcare (Mutual Aid Diabetes, n.d.).

Healthcare Access and Quality

Healthcare access in the United States is crucial for adequate and quality care. However, forty-three percent of adults eligible to work in the United States need to be more adequately insured, meaning they either need coverage, have a gap in coverage, or the insurance does not meet their needs (Collins et al., 2022). According to one survey conducted by the Commonwealth Fund Biennial Health Insurance Survey, forty-six percent of individuals stated that they had skipped or delayed care due to costs, and forty-two percent admitted to having problems paying off medical bills. The survey also revealed that the people who were uninsured for more than a year were young, poor, sicker, living in the South, and typically Latinx (Collins et al., 2022).

There was a time when I volunteered at Benioff Children's Hospital in Oakland as a navigator at the FIND desk, the acronym for Family Information and Navigation Desk. The purpose was to assist families with social service needs to free up a doctor's time to see patients. As a navigator, I handed out diapers, food, preschool applications, and referrals for housing. There was a wide gamut of requests amongst families, yet what was consistent was the relationship that occurs between health needs and economic standing. Many clients needed a computer or a car, two essential items for quickly finding housing, researching school enrollment requirements, or easily getting to a supermarket versus utilizing a nearby stop-and-shop with less healthy options.

Those who do not have economic security tend to fare worse than those who do. In contrast, many who face severe health circumstances end up financially vulnerable. Close to 53,000 families have become bankrupt yearly due to high medical expenses and bills (Konish, 2019). Research has shown that one in four Americans is in debt due to medical bills despite the Affordable Care Act being passed by Congress in 2010. Most expenses are attributable to hospital bills, prescription costs, insurance deductibles and premiums, and loss of wages due to health-related circumstances. This dire reality leaves medically vulnerable people choosing life-saving supplies over necessities such as housing, food, and heat (Bielenberg, 2021). This precarious decision-making has left many people with health conditions without a home.

Inspired by a 1942 report by the British academic and civil servant William Beveridge, who identified what he termed "giant evils" that needed to be overcome for a peaceful and prosperous society, a 2016 report that was conducted by The Brookings Institute sighted healthcare as one of the "five giant evils" that create poverty in the United States; other factors that precipitate poverty include low household income, limited education, concentrated spatial poverty, and unemployment. In their research, The Brookings Institute found that poverty impacted 60 percent of a person's overall health (Reeves et al., 2016). In contrast, today, healthcare expenses account for 66 percent of bankruptcies in America (Konish, 2019).

Without health insurance and quality care, people typically do not have a primary care physician advocating for them. Fewer tests are conducted, less consistent care is provided, and preventative maintenance is obsolete (U.S. Department of Health and Human Services, n.d.). These circumstances result in worse outcomes than those with adequate insurance and a regular doctor. Furthermore, the Kaiser Family Foundation reports that uninsured individuals pay for up to half of their care out-of-pocket. To make matters worse, hospitals typically charge uninsured patients higher rates than insured individuals (Tolbert et al., 2020), upward of two to four times more than those who are insured pay (Kissell, 2022).

Ironically, many states charge individuals a fee for not having health insurance. This expense feels like a cruel loop that already vulnerable people must face. Without health insurance through employment, many cannot afford private insurance, resulting in a tax penalty in many states. For instance, California charges individuals up to $800 per adult and $400 per dependent for not having health insurance, whereas New Jersey charges $695 (Kissell, 2022). However, only some qualify for public assistance. This creates a harsh economic punishment for those who are already struggling. Despite Congress eliminating this federal penalty, several states have mandates and requirements.

There are many reasons individuals do not have health insurance. From my volunteer vantage point, I saw migrant families coming into the clinic who feared asking for help, single mothers working multiple part-time jobs that did not offer insurance, and loving families who fell between the cracks of affording a policy yet not qualifying for government assistance. The Kaiser Family Foundation found that 73.7% of individuals are uninsured due to the high costs of health coverage despite the Affordable Care Act being passed in 2010 (Artiga, 2018). Many people do not have access to health insurance through a job, and financial assistance is not available to those living in states with limited Medicaid coverage. Also included in the uninsured are undocumented immigrants who do not qualify for Medicaid or Marketplace insurance coverage (Tolbert et al., 2020). Moreover, while formerly incarcerated populations qualify for government-assisted healthcare, many do not know it is available or how to apply for it. Beyond being unable to access health insurance, several additional circumstances fall under the umbrella of social determinants of health.

Education Access and Quality

Research has shown that higher levels of education equate to a better quality of health care, and people in this demographic tend to live longer. Moreover, children growing up in low-income families and those who experience social determinants of health are more likely to struggle with school subjects such as math and reading. They are also less likely to graduate from high school and rarely attend college (U.S. Department of Health and Human Services, n.d.). Research conducted by the University of Massachusetts Global revealed that higher levels of education lead to benefits rarely considered, such as lower crime rates, community involvement, and improved self-care. Furthermore, the study revealed seven benefits of having a high educational status, which include:

1. Living longer
2. Less economic and occupational stress
3. Lower rates of smoking

4.   Fewer common illnesses
5.   Fewer mental health struggles
6.   Better diets and exercise habits
7.   More likely to have health insurance
     (University of Massachusetts Global, n.d.).

Higher education levels show decreased mortality rates related to social and behavioral risk factors across all age, gender, and racial groups. Within the United States, individuals with at least seventeen years of education have a 93 percent lower mortality rate than those with eleven years of education or less. The main contributors of death for the less educated include preventable causes such as lung cancer, respiratory diseases, homicide, and accidents (University of Massachusetts Global, n.d.). Those with higher levels of education experience fewer stressors, making them less likely to adopt unhealthy habits as a coping mechanism, such as smoking, drugs, and unhealthy diets.

Research has revealed that increased levels of college education reduce rates of cancer and cardiovascular diseases (Tulane University, 2021), such as heart conditions, diabetes, hypertension and asthma (University of Massachusetts Global, n.d.). In one study, thirteen percent of participants with a high school degree or less died prematurely compared to five percent of those with a college degree (Tulane University, 2021). Yet the cause and effect can run in both directions. Those with poor health are less likely to pursue higher education, yet those with compromised health at a young age may be motivated to focus on healthier options regardless of educational levels (Frakt, 2019).

Incarcerated individuals "overwhelmingly come from disadvantaged socioeconomic backgrounds" and experience low levels of formal education and increased rates of chronic health conditions (Sheehan, 2018, para. 2). The Sentencing Project found that adolescents who are incarcerated have higher rates of poor health and shortened lifespans as adults and suffer "disproportionately from many physical health challenges" that include dental, vision, and hearing issues (Mendel, 2023, para. 8). Unfortunately, many studies on chronic health outcomes typically exclude incarcerated populations in their data, and therefore, it's challenging to get accurate statistics. However, what is known is the correlation between socioeconomic backgrounds, education levels, and the relationship between health outcomes (Sheehan, 2018).

For my doctoral research I interviewed incarcerated women living with diabetes. It is worth noting that the number of incarcerated women in the United States has steadily increased over the past forty years, with women's state prison populations growing by 834% in that time. More than twice the growth of men's state prisons (Sawyer, 2018). Most women enter the correctional system due to "life changes such as poverty, unemployment, and significant physical or behavioral health struggles." Furthermore, many women who are incarcerated are women of color and come from impoverished backgrounds. Eighty percent of women detained in U.S. jails are mothers (Kajstura, 2019), and 60% incarcerated in state prisons have a child (Equal Justice Initiative, Incarceration of Women is Growing Twice as Fast as that of Men, 2018). These statistics contribute to fewer resources to gain reliable employment and access adequate health insurance.

The circumstances that women inside prison walls face are reflective of life within the general population of society. One woman I interviewed acknowledged that most women would not request to see a doctor unless the situation was dire. Instead, they chose to save money for toiletries and hygienic products. "So you have a choice. Either get your hygiene right, or you go to medical. A lot of us here, like, forget it unless I'm practically dying" (H. Laura, personal communication, May 8, 2020). For a chronic condition such as diabetes, that choice can be deadly. Audra K. reinforced the issues with the copay system that Laura H. had mentioned, commenting that the medical personnel will see a prisoner if she does not have credit on the books, but "you make a couple of dollars on their little bullshit jobs, you're not going to see a dime of it cause it's going to medical which is not really helping you anyway" (H. Laura, personal communication, May 8, 2020).

FIGURE 3   *Linda*[1]
PHOTOGRAPH: SARA BENNETT, 2019

FIGURE 4   *Linda at home*[2]
PHOTOGRAPH: SARA BENNETT, 2022

Once released, many women face additional financial hardships if they do not have family support. After twenty-five years of incarceration due to the three-strikes laws in California, Regina M. was the first female "three-striker" to be found suitable for release by the parole board. Regina, born in Cuba, described the difficulties she has experienced since being released in July 2020. Despite not being at risk for deportation, she has had difficulty accessing the documents needed to find employment, a job, and apply for general relief.

Social and Community Context

Access to options and choices is crucial to educational and health-related outcomes. A vital part of that outcome is a solid foundation consisting of social networks, community, and personal relationships that provide positive influences. Social health is a crucial part of the overall well-being of individuals, especially those with compromised living environments – such as living a life behind prison walls. Positive relationships with neighbors and others within the community reduce rates of isolation, depression, and anxiety. Furthermore, research shows that healthier people have increased rates of civic engagement, including voting, feeling more connected to their communities, and experiencing an increase in agency over the well-being and improvement of their surroundings (Salinsky, 2022).

Results from local surveys provide more insight into the activities and social support that affect people's health outcomes. The Rural Health Information Hub is one resource that provides data on rural communities. Specifically, they are addressing civic participation, discrimination, incarceration, and social connectedness (The Rural Health Information Hub, n.d.). Other studies reflect how the interpersonal networks between the community and neighbors, including social activities, affect people's physical and mental health. Medical professionals and sociologists can utilize these outcomes to assist individuals and develop solutions for community health policies and programs (Knapp & Hall, 2018).

One approach that is being used to address social determinants of health is asset-based community development (ABCD). This approach utilizes the assets that already exist within a community. By leveraging existing resources, experts, organizations, and physical attributes such as land and natural resources, the ABCD directs positive changes and addresses social determinants of health within the community (The Rural Health Information Hub, n.d.).

In the book Youth Violence Prevention Through Asset-based Community Development, the author, Pedro R. Payne, presents a background on asset-based community development and the dependence on government agencies. These agencies typically implement programs that are "needs-driven" as a way to address issues such as inadequate housing, youth violence, and substance abuse issues. These "needs" are assessed with surveys conducted by government officials and target the areas they deem most in need (Payne, 2006, p. 25).

Overlooked through this process are the existing resources that are in place, thus creating desperation and despair within the community. Individuals who live in these neighborhoods come to believe that their only resources are the service providers that are recommended by previously mentioned agencies. Community members in need become the "customers" of these service providers, ultimately finding themselves dependent on the government and local non-profit organizations (Payne, 2006, p. 26).

Another element that impacts individuals struggling with financial vulnerability is violence. Between 2018 and 2012, individuals who lived in households below the poverty level experienced twice the rate of violent victimization than those in higher financial brackets (American Academy of Family Physicians, n.d.). The violence and victimization lead to compromised health outcomes. The United States has some of the highest rates of childhood poverty in the world and some of the poorest health outcomes, both of which can lead to high incarceration rates (Anonymous, 2023).

Economic Stability

While the social and community context of health determinants is critical, especially for an individual's emotional well-being, economic stability provides a foundation for all areas of a person's well-being. It is through financial security that a person can have adequate food, safe housing, and steady employment, yet 1 in 10 people live in poverty (Semega et al., 2018). Individuals with disabilities, injuries, or severe conditions are more vulnerable to unemployment and poverty. Yet, even gainfully employed people can only sometimes afford the necessary items to stay healthy (U.S. Department of Health and Human Services, n.d.).

The economic outcomes for those living in rural areas proved different for people living in metropolitan environments. In 2018, statistics showed employment rates to be higher in rural areas in addition to slower job growth. Furthermore, poverty rates within rural areas tend to be higher than in more populated urban spaces (The Rural Health Information Hub, n.d.), which is consistent with the education level for those living in urban areas versus rural

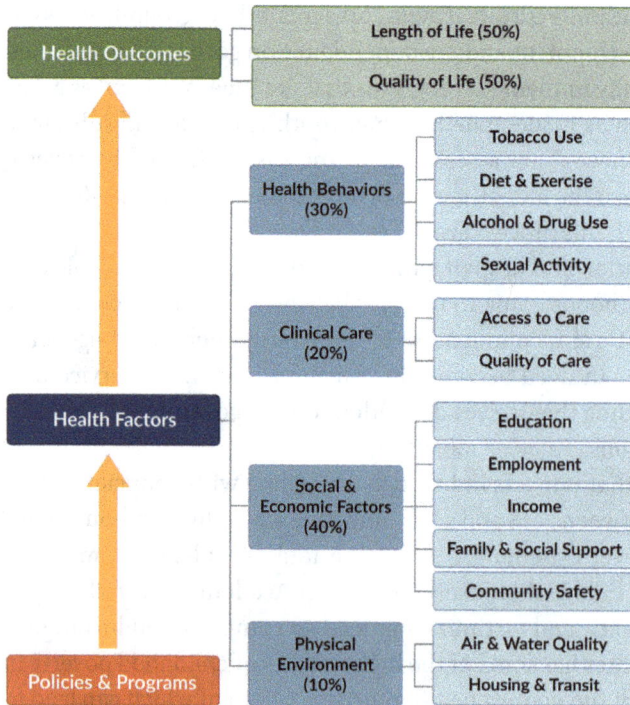

FIGURE 5   The University of Wisconsin Population Health Institute (Source: County Health Rankings & Roadmaps, 2024. www.countyhealthrankings.org)

communities. The rate of individuals with a bachelor's degree or higher living in cities is still considerably higher than those within rural areas (U.S. Department of Agriculture, 2024).

A lack of economic stability impacts an individual's ability to see a doctor, have consistency with prescriptions, and have access to specialists. However, the problem goes beyond access to medications and healthcare providers. Stress is a primary factor affecting health outcomes for those in lower financial brackets. Continually negotiating financial pressure while making healthy lifestyle decisions can dramatically impact overall health. According to Julie Kalkowski, founder and executive director of the Financial Hope Collective, social scientists refer to this phenomenon as the "limited resource model of self-control" (White et al., 2019, para. 2).

The idea behind this concept is that an individual with few resources typically has limited energy to govern behavior. For example, someone working multiple jobs who is stressed about financial circumstances might sleep less. The lack of sleep, therefore, makes it more challenging to concentrate on healthy habits such as eating healthy and exercising.

Neighborhood and Built Environment

Where people live impacts their health outcomes almost as much as what they put into their bodies. Research discussing the potential of neighborhood interventions shows improved health and reduced health inequities. Several categories describe the environments that impact health: environmental exposure to elements such as air pollution; physical spaces such as walkability, parks, green space, and outdoor recreational options; and social environments that include community connections and violence (Roux, 2016).

Social environments are incredibly important to newly released individuals re-entering society after incarceration. According to Dr. Shira Shavit, incarceration is not only about locking people up for indeterminate amounts of time; "it is also about what happens when people leave those systems and return to their communities" (Weiner, 2023, para. 16). There is also the issue of getting adequate referrals to doctors and health specialists and getting people to trust others upon their release. Having strong ties within a community can assist with that.

According to Dr. Rob Kahn, the Executive Lead for the Michael Fisher Child Health Equity Center in Cincinnati, Ohio, multi general, structural disinvestment in neighborhoods exists and contributes to poor health outcomes. Circumstances such as a lack of local, decent paying jobs, high renterships with out-of-town landlords, and no groceries or enough money to put food on the table all factor in. These components combined create a cumulative array that predicts who will not be kindergarten-ready and will have high rates of asthma and other health and social challenges, in addition to an increased vulnerability to incarceration (M.D. Rob Kahn, personal communication, May 23, 2023).

Redlining is an age-old term that refers to the "historic race-based exclusionary tactics in real estate" (Jackson, 2021) that barred Black citizens from buying homes. This practice has had a ripple effect on communities today. The term refers to the color-coded maps of government homeownership programs created in the 1930s and continued through the Civil Rights Movement. These programs provided government-insured mortgages to prevent foreclosures from happening in the wake of the Depression. Neighborhoods were categorized based on their level of riskiness, "A" through "D," with "D" being deemed as the least desirable and most likely to go down in value. This was also the neighborhood where most Black residents lived. Therefore, this "D" neighborhood received a red line that fenced in the region. Redlining impacted more

FIGURE 6   Grass-fed (pork)[3]
             PAINTING: SHANEQUA BENITEZ, 2023

than 200 cities across the United States and created a dynamic that made it difficult for those residents to have financial security, adequate food sources, stable educational systems, and health centers – all critical elements of social determinants of health (Jackson, 2021).

Diet and Exercise

In impoverished neighborhoods, proximity to supermarkets that offer fresh produce and healthy options is lacking, leaving residents to rely on small convenience stores that stock an inventory of highly processed, unhealthy items. This creates what the United States Department of Agriculture refers to as a food desert. Food insecurity, which encapsulates food deserts, impacted over eleven percent of the population in 2022. Access to healthy food can be difficult, but affording these options dramatically affects the health of communities.

Food insecurity has been attributed to compromised health outcomes such as obesity and chronic diseases, as well as affecting mental health. Research has shown that food insecurity creates and contributes to stress and anxiety, which further exacerbates mental health and chronic health conditions. In the fall of 2022, The White House had its first conference on food, nutrition, and health in 53 years to end hunger and increase healthy eating in the United States by 2030. As stated by the U.S. Health and Human Services Assistant Secretary for Health Admiral Rachel L. Levine, "No one should wonder where their next meal is coming from, or if they will have a safe opportunity to be physically active" (Miller, 2022, para. 17).

Food insecurity is most impactful on single-parent households, and Black and Hispanic households. In 2021, more than thirty percent of households had incomes below the Federal poverty line resulting in food insecurity (U.S. Department of Agriculture, 2024). Despite its overall wealth as a country, the United States has higher rates of food insecurity than many other developed countries. Unlike other countries, most individuals within the United States rely on commercial entities for the food supply. Furthermore, the United States has an average diet that consists of an unhealthy diet of "excess salt, saturated fat, refined grains, calories from solid fats and added sugars. Americans also eat fewer vegetables, fruits, whole grains, dairy products, and oils than recommended" (Reinberg, 2023, para. 3). Healthy food options tend to be more expensive than processed food and therefore the financial impact of health comes into play once again.

I recently had the opportunity to travel to Peru, and the definition of poverty is quite different from developed countries. Many people live in homes that would be considered substandard in the United States. However, there are no hungry or homeless individuals. Each person within an area contributes to the greater community, in addition to a bartering system that ensures that each person has what they need. It's a very one-for-all and all-for-one way of living. The community serves as an extended family that takes care of one another.

In Peru, and many countries within South America, people rely on food from crops and livestock. These items not only nourish their families and communities but also contribute to a bartering system in smaller pueblos (small towns or villages) to trade different crops and supplies with others. Ultimately, there may be little financial abundance, but everyone has what they need. The larger cities have markets where local fruits, vegetables, grains, and various meats are sold at varied prices to ensure that everyone is able to adequately feed their families.

FIGURE 7   Peru market
PHOTOGRAPH: WHITE, 2023

This sense of community and the low rates of incarceration are in stark contrast to correlations between social problems, community and incarceration that occur in the United States. The U.S. rates at the top of the global list for most people incarcerated with over two million people behind bars, whereas Peru, with ten percent of the population of the United States, has just over ninety thousand incarcerated (World Population Review, n.d.), however Peru's crime rates have been steadily increasing in the larger cities versus smaller farming communities where family and neighbors are connected and supportive of one another (Country Reports, n.d.).

Homelessness

Homelessness is another catastrophic outcome of health conditions due to the immense financial burden that is placed on people. University of Washington student Jessica Bielenberg conducted a research study for her Master's thesis, revealing that unpaid medical bills were the primary reason for extended homelessness for up to two years. Furthermore, it has been shown that homelessness is a medical risk. Despite an average age span of 80 in the United States, a study at the Boston Health Care for the Homeless Program revealed that the average lifespan for those living on the streets was between 42 and 52 years (Hayashi, 2016).

Individuals living on the street or in unstable housing may be predisposed to worse conditions and experience food insecurity; those who are living with chronic illnesses and diseases face additional hardships, such as people with diabetes who do not have a place to store insulin, or have access to medical supplies. Also making the situation difficult are the remote and challenging places where the homeless population resides, making transportation to medical services complex (Schrag, 2014). As pointed out by journalist Seiji Hayashi, "The sick and vulnerable become homeless, and the homeless become sicker and more vulnerable" (Miller, 2022). It is a toxic, cyclical problem that feeds upon itself, and according to data from *The Wall Street Journal*, there has been an increase in homelessness since funding and support due to the COVID-19 pandemic dried up as the virus faded (Kamp, 2023).

Incarceration

Incarceration is a social determinant that impacts health, along with the location of where people are born, grow, live, and work. Most prisoners are from poor neighborhoods and tend to be individuals of color who are given sentences far more severe than their white counterparts. In the past forty years, the incarceration of individuals in the United States has increased by 500 percent (Brown & Patterson, 2016). Many of the arrests are due to the three strike laws and mandatory drug sentencing. In 1994 California voters enacted the "Three Strikes and You are Out" law. This new law "imposed a life sentence for almost any crime, no matter how minor, if the defendant had two prior convictions for crimes defined as serious or violent by the California Penal Code" (Stanford Law School, n.d.). Today, due to the three-strikes law, more than half of incarcerated individuals are serving life sentences for non-violent crimes.

The rates of chronic illness amongst currently and formerly incarcerated individuals are above the average rates of non-incarcerated populations. Yet, these health complications also impact the individual and the communities from which they come. Families of incarcerated people are affected by "community fragmentation and disruption of family ties that negatively impact mental and familial health." Furthermore, the death rates of newly released people are 12.7 times higher than the general, non-incarcerated population. The reasons for this include violence, drug overdoses, and a lapse in treatment of chronic health issues for which they were receiving medication in prison (Peterson & Brinkley-Rubenstein, 2021).

I interviewed Laura H. in 2020, who was diagnosed with type 2 diabetes during the last three years of her sentence, and she stated that her diabetes is much more stable now that she has been released. She believes that the

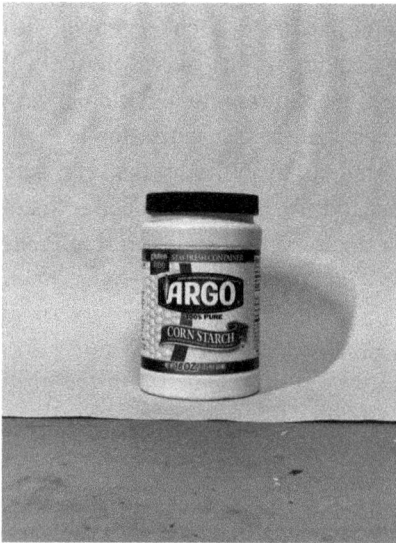

FIGURE 8
It's the starch[5]
PHOTOGRAPH: WHITE, 2020

FIGURE 9   Stigma(ta)[4]
PAINTING: ZEPH VONDENHUEVEL

food choices in prison contributed to her diagnosis because "in prison, it's the starch and stuff. The food they give us" (H. Laura, personal communication, 2020). Furthermore, Laura H. now appreciates her ability to have water when she wants it because it was not readily available in prison but was instead mostly provided during meals. Now that she is no longer incarcerated, she can breathe better, and her A1C is much lower. An A1C score is the average blood sugar reading for someone living with diabetes. It is typically taken every three months during medical check-ups.

One recommendation for solving the dilemma of unstable medical care inside prison walls is to have an outside entity compile data and monitor all facilities in the United States. The Centers for Disease Control reports on other social determinants of health, including "chronic disease indicators, minority health disparities, and regions with high poverty rates" (Peterson & Brinkley-Rubenstein, 2021). Monitoring incarceration as a social determinant of health would provide invaluable data and increase the public's confidence in the system.

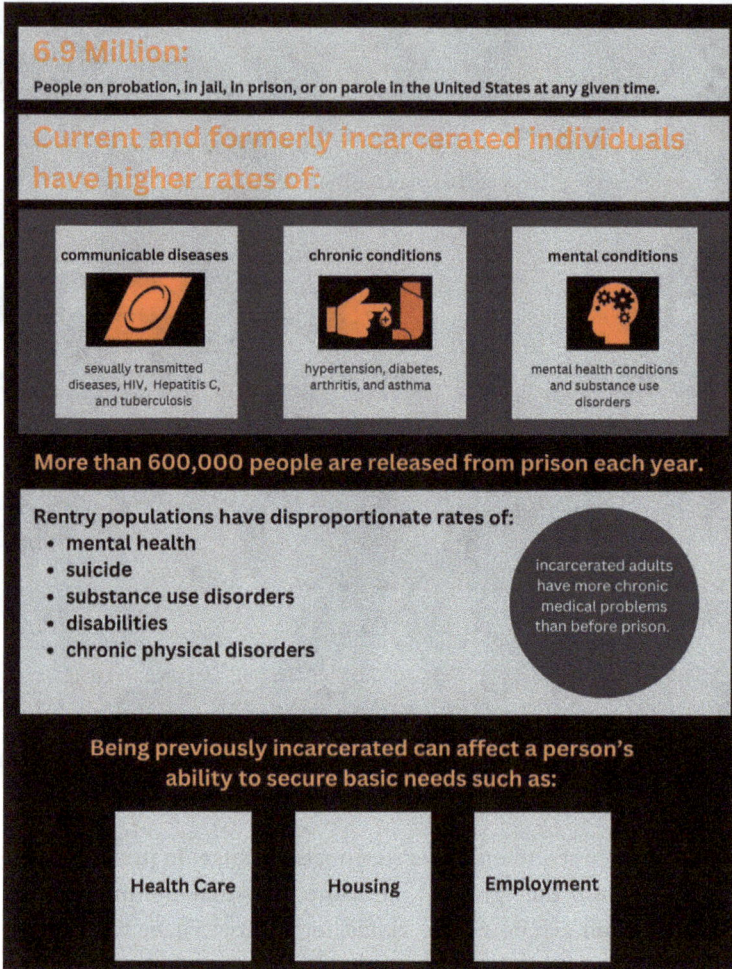

6.9 Million:
People on probation, in jail, in prison, or on parole in the United States at any given time.

Current and formerly incarcerated individuals have higher rates of:

communicable diseases	chronic conditions	mental conditions
sexually transmitted diseases, HIV, Hepatitis C, and tuberculosis	hypertension, diabetes, arthritis, and asthma	mental health conditions and substance use disorders

More than 600,000 people are released from prison each year.

Rentry populations have disproportionate rates of:
- **mental health**
- **suicide**
- **substance use disorders**
- **disabilities**
- **chronic physical disorders**

incarcerated adults have more chronic medical problems than before prison.

Being previously incarcerated can affect a person's ability to secure basic needs such as:

Health Care	Housing	Employment

FIGURE 10   Public Health Issues of Incarceration based on data from The National Institute for Health Care Management (NIHCM) Foundation (Current and formerly incarcerated individuals have significantly higher rates of chronic health conditions. White, 2024)

Interventions

As pointed out, social determinants of health are a combination of circumstances and a multi-determined set of factors that impact health outcomes for millions of individuals yearly.

It has become increasingly apparent to those working in public health sectors that health equity must become a priority to improve the health of communities impacted by social determinants, including incarceration. To do so, non-health sector considerations, such as education, living environments, financial security, and more, must be examined to address these inequitable situations (Artiga, 2018).

Examples of solutions include considering how "the availability and accessibility of public transportation affects access to employment, affordable healthy foods, health care, and other important drivers of health and wellness" (Artiga, 2018). Additionally, reducing food deserts in low-income communities, providing healthy meal plans in schools, developing community gardens to encourage "production and consumption of healthy foods," and using art to bring forth awareness and information (Artiga, 2018).

However, it is more complex than just healthy food options. Dr. Robert Kahn points out that "it's never just about food. No family ever says I'm really hungry and I love my four-bedroom home. It is complicated and connected yet we operate in silos" (M.D. Rob Kahn, personal communication, May 23, 2023). Khan, who is the Executive Lead at the Michael Fisher Child Health Equity Center, points out their plan to help organizations, including healthcare organizations, be more effective through three steps:

1. Find the social needs and connect them to an organization.
2. Assist organizations to be their best and most effective.
3. Move upstream to the issues to assist in changing policies and standards.

Kahn explains the political economy of illness, describing how organizations are preoccupied with the issues downstream, and noting that incarceration will always be downstream- no one is looking upstream at what's causing the problems.

Many states are now considering a "Health in All Policies" approach that "identifies the ways in which decisions in multiple sectors affect health, and how improved health can support the goals of these multiple sectors" (Artiga, 2018, para. 5). The model brings together partners from diverse sectors to promote job creation, provide transportation access, and improve educational opportunities (Artiga, 2018).

One solution to bridging the social challenge gap is having patients entering healthcare facilities fill out a survey identifying their needs, such as food, assistance with school enrollment, resources for housing, employment, and legal help. These difficult topics can be destigmatized when asked in private and without judgment by a caring provider. Understanding the patient's situation allows for a more thorough assessment of health needs and the determinants that impact an individual's stability (Andermann, 2016).

Notes

1   *LINDA*, 70, in the rec room for the medically unemployed at Taconic Correctional Facility
    (2019)
    Sentence: 30 years to life
    Incarcerated at the age of 43 in 1992
    "This is my 27th year being incarcerated. I've been scared, lonely, hurt, disappointed and
    forgotten. When I got here 11 months ago, I couldn't believe all the women I had done time
    with were still here going to Board after Board, and never getting out. Will that happen to me?
    I do my hair and makeup every day. It makes me feel good. But on the inside, I'm breaking
    down. To name a few, I had a triple bypass, 2 strokes, major back surgery, and I take 30 pills a
    day. The bottom line is—I beg for forgiveness and a second chance. Will I ever see my free-
    dom????? Will I die behind these walls??????????"

2   *LINDA*, 74, in a transitional house she shares with 7 other women, 6 weeks after her release
    Queens, NY (2022)
    Sentence: 30 years to life. Served: 30 years. Released: October 2022
    "I'M FREE!! I almost didn't make it. But I had a will to live. My last year I got COVID-19, was in
    and out of the hospital and lived on the medical unit called Long Term Care. After my long,
    hard 30 years, I didn't get to walk out... but was taken out in a wheelchair. And 9 days later,
    due to improper medication and a leaking valve, I landed in the hospital. I wanted so badly
    to make it out alive and I did... I'M FREE!!"

3   When creating this piece, I thought of the slaves that worked in fields. When it came time to
    eat dinner the slaves were left with the scraps of the animals. These were the parts like ribs,
    bacon, pig feet, and chitlins just to make a few. What people working the fields did was turn
    the most undesirable parts of the animals into cultural staples. When I was thinking about
    the connection with redlining one word came to mind: "access"! People that live in redlined
    areas simply don't have access to quality meats and vegetables. This isn't by accident but
    simply by design. Grocery stores that hold & sell high quality foods make choices not to
    have their stores in black and brown communities. This piece shows a pig in the window of
    a butcher's market. The sign reads "grass-fed" quality scraps. The connection Is that even the
    "quality" meats in redlined communities are still the scraps compared to the quality meats in
    the suburbs. This is the sibling piece to Grass-fed scraps(beef).

4   "*Stigma(ta)*" is a mixed media painting depicting a self-portrait of the artist in shackles, with
    their hands up in the air, the words 'Kill Me' burnt into the palms. Surrounding the subject
    are pill bottles, syringes, cockroaches, and sticky notes showing the faces of the pain scales
    typically seen in doctors' offices. This piece is representative of the stigma, both internalized
    and encountered by those who are incarcerated or are formerly incarcerated, and those who
    are recovering addicts, especially in regard to receiving healthcare and dealing with chronic
    illnesses and chronic pain in this country.

5   Argo corn starch with paper background, digital photograph. The photo represents the high-
    starch foods frequently found in prisons.

References

Andermann, A. (2016, December 6). Taking action on the social determinants of
    health in clinical practice: A framework for health professionals. *Canadian Medical
    Association Journal*, 17–18. https://doi.org/10.1503/cmaj.160177

Artiga, S. (2018, May 10). *Beyond health care: The role of social determinants in promoting health and health equity.* Kaiser Family Foundation. https://www.kff.org/racial-equity-and-health-policy/issue-brief/beyond-health-care-the-role-of-social-determinants-in-promoting-health-and-health-equity/

Avendano, M., & Kawachi, I. (2014, January 9). *Why do Americans have shorter life expectancy and worse health than people in higher-income countries? Annual Review of Public Health.* https://www.ncbi.nlm.nih.gov/pmc/articles/PMC4112220/

Becker, S., & Alexander, L. (2016). *ReThink health at The Ripple Foundation.* https://www.rethinkhealth.org/wp-content/uploads/2016/04/ReThink-Health-March-17-Report-1.pdf

Bielenberg, J. (2021, August, 23). *Medical debt and homelessness. Public Health Post.* https://www.publichealthpost.org/research/medical-debt-homelessness/

Brown, T. N., & Patterson, E. (2016, June 28). Wounds from incarceration that never heal. *The New Republic.* https://newrepublic.com/article/134712/wounds-incarceration-never-heal

Collins, S. R., Haynes, L. A., & Masitha, R. (2022, September 29). The state of U.S. health insurance in 2022. *The Commonwealth Fund.* https://www.commonwealthfund.org/sites/default/files/2022-09/Collins_state_of_coverage_biennial_survey_2022_db.pdf

Country Reports. (n.d.). *Crime information for tourists in Peru.* https://www.countryreports.org/country/Peru/crimes.htm

Equal Justice Initiative. (2018, May 11). *Incarceration of women is growing twice as fast as that of men.* https://eji.org/news/female-incarceration-growing-twice-as-fast-as-male-incarceration

Frakt, A. (2019, June 3). Does your education level affect your health. *New York Times.* https://www.nytimes.com/2019/06/03/upshot/education-impact-health-longevity.html

Hayashi, S. (2016, January 25). How health and homelessness are connected – Medically. *The Atlantic.* https://www.theatlantic.com/politics/archive/2016/01/how-health-and-homelessness-are-connectedmedically/458871/

Jackson, C. (2021, August 17). What is redlining? *The New York Times.* https://www.nytimes.com/2021/08/17/realestate/what-is-redlining.html

Kajstura, A. (2019, October 29). Women's mass incarceration: The whole pie. 2019. *Prison Policy Initiative.* https://www.prisonpolicy.org/reports/pie2019women.html

Kamp, J. (2023, August 14). More Americans are ending up homeless – At a record rate. *Wall Street Journal.* https://www.wsj.com/articles/homelessness-increasing-united-states-housing-costs-e1990ac7

Kissell, C. (2022, November 3). What happens if you don't have health insurance? *Forbes Advisor.* https://www.forbes.com/advisor/health-insurance/what-happens-if-you-dont-have-health-insurance/

Knapp, T., & Hall, L. (2018, July 6). The social determinants of health in a community context: Lessons for sociological practice. *Journal of Applied Social Science*. https://doi.org/10.1177/1936724418785413

Konish, L. (2019, February 11). This is the real reason most Americans file for Bankruptcy. *CNBC. Personal Finance.* https://www.cnbc.com/2019/02/11/this-is-the-real-reason-most-americans-file-for-bankruptcy.html

Mendel, R. (2023, March 1). Why youth incarceration fails: An updated review on the evidence. *The Sentencing Project.* sentencingproject.org/reports/why-youth-incarceration-fails-an-updated-review-of-the-evidence/

Miller, N. S. (2022, September 27). Food insecurity and food deserts in the US: A research roundup and explainer. *The Journalist's Resource.* https://journalistsresource.org/home/food-insecurity-health/

Mutual Aid Diabetes. (n.d.). https://mutualaiddiabetes.com/about-mad/

Osmick, M. D., Jane, M., & Wilson, M. (2020, January 13). Social determinants of health—Relevant history, A call to action, An organization's transformational story, and what can employers do? *American Journal of Health Promotion.* https://journals.sagepub.com/doi/10.1177/0890117119896122d#bibr1-0890117119896122d

Payne, P. R. (2006). *Youth violence prevention through asset-based community development.* LFB Scholarly Publishing.

Peterson, M., & Brinkley-Rubinstein, L. (2021, October 19). Incarceration is a health threat. Why isn't it monitored like one? *Health Affairs Forefront.* https://www.healthaffairs.org/content/forefront/incarceration-health-threat-why-isn-t-monitored-like-one

Reeves, R., Rodrigue, E., & Kneebone, E. (2016, April). Five evils: Multidimensional poverty and race in America. *The Brookings Institute.* https://www.brookings.edu/wp-content/uploads/2016/06/reeveskneebonerodrigue_multidimensionalpoverty_fullpaper.pdf

Reinberg, S. (2023, January 17). Why is American food so unhealthy. *U.S. News and World Report.* https://www.usnews.com/news/health-news/articles/2023-01-17/why-is-american-food-so-unhealthy

Roux, A. V. D. (2016, March). Neighborhoods and health: What do we know? What should we do? *American Journal of Public Health, 106*(3), 430–431. https://www.ncbi.nlm.nih.gov/pmc/articles/PMC4815954/

Salinsky, E. (2022, April). Civic engagement is a social determinant of health. *Grant Makers in Health.* https://www.gih.org/publication/civic-engagement-is-a-social-determinant-of-health/

Sawyer, W. (2018, January 9). The gender divide: Tracking women's state prison growth. *Prison Policy Initiative.* https://www.prisonpolicy.org/reports/women_overtime.html

Schrag, J. (2014, October 24). The social determinants of health: Homelessness and unemployment. *America's Essential Hospitals.* https://www.coursesidekick.com/health-science/2176169

Semega, J., Kollar, M., Creamer, J., & Mohanty, A. (2021). Income and poverty in the United States: 2018. U.S. Department of Commerce. U.S. Census Bureau. census.gov/content/dam/Census/library/publications/2019/demo/p60-266.pdf

Sheehan, C. M. (2018, October 16). Education and health conditions among the currently incarcerated and the non-incarcerated populations. *Population Research and Policy Review,* 73–93. https://www.ncbi.nlm.nih.gov/pmc/articles/PMC9974178/

Stanford Law School. (n.d.). Three strikes basics. *Three Strikes Project.* https://law.stanford.edu/stanford-justice-advocacy-project/three-strikes-basics/

The Rural Health Information Hub. (n.d.). *Asset-based community approaches.* https://www.ruralhealthinfo.org/toolkits/sdoh/2/social-and-community-context/asset-based

Tolbert, J., Orgera, K., & Damico, A. (2020, November 6). *Key facts about the uninsured population.* Kaiser Family Foundation. https://www.kff.org/uninsured/issue-brief/key-facts-about-the-uninsured-population/

Tulane University. (2021, January 27). *Education as a social determinant of health.* https://publichealth.tulane.edu/blog/social-determinant-of-health-education-is-crucial/

University of Massachusetts Global. (n.d.). Education and health: 7 ways learning leads to healthy living. https://www.umassglobal.edu/news-and-events/blog/5-ways-education-leads-to-healthy-living

U.S. Department of Agriculture. (2024, July 22). *Economic research service.* Food Security and Nutrition Assistance. https://www.ers.usda.gov/data-products/ag-and-food-statistics-charting-the-essentials/food-security-and-nutrition-assistance/

U.S. Department of Health and Human Services. (n.d.). Office of disease prevention and health promotion. "Social Determinants of Health." *Healthy People 2030.* https://health.gov/healthypeople/priority-areas/social-determinants-health

Weiner, S. (2023, January 10). Out of prison but struggling to stay healthy. *AAMC News.* https://www.aamc.org/news/out-prison-struggling-stay-healthy

White, N. D., Packard, K., & Kalkowski, J. (2019). Financial education and coaching: A lifestyle medicine approach to addressing financial stress. *American Journal of Lifestyle Medicine,* 540–543. https://www.ncbi.nlm.nih.gov/pmc/articles/PMC6796220/

Wilkinson, R., & Marmot, M. (2003) *Social determinants of health. The solid facts.* World Health Organization.

World Population Review. (2024). *Incarceration rates by country 2024.* https://worldpopulationreview.com/country-rankings/incarceration-rates-by-country

CHAPTER 2

Chronic Illness and Diabetes

> As we struggle to ensure that high quality chronic disease treatment
> becomes the norm for patients in carceral settings, we must simul-
> taneously not lose sight of the equal need to focus on optimizing
> health through access to meaningful exercise, healthy food, and
> mental healthcare.
>
> DR. BRIE WILLIAMS

∴

Explaining why we were not requesting a special Disneyland pass to skip the lines, I once told my daughter that diabetes was not a disability. At the time, I believed I was instilling a sense of strength and normalcy while discouraging the use of her diagnosis as a crutch. Naively, I overlooked the fact that diabetes is a chronic, debilitating, and life-threatening disease that can be overwhelming and exhausting to manage day in and out.

Chronic disease is a medically ubiquitous term that encapsulates numerous conditions. The Center for Disease Control labels heart disease, stroke, cancer, type 2 diabetes, obesity, and arthritis as a chronic disease, whereas The Centers for Medicare and Medicaid Services have a more extensive list of conditions, including Alzheimer's disease, depression, and HIV. These differences can create confusion and misunderstandings and impact costs and solutions (Bernell & Howard, 2016). The World Health Organization defines *chronic disease* as "being of long duration, generally slow in progression and not passed from person to person" (Reynolds et al., 2018, para. 5). Furthermore, chronic diseases require extended management, supervision, and observation periods. According to the U.S. National Center for Health Statistics, an illness is considered chronic if it lasts more than three months (Chaffey, 2021).

Chronic disease and chronic illness are two terms frequently used interchangeably. Chronic disease defines the biomedical classification of the condition. In contrast, chronic illness speaks to the personal experience of living with the side effects and affliction of the chronic condition (Martin, 2007). Chronic illnesses currently affect fifty percent of the population and are expected to impact 164 million Americans by the year 2025 (Edwards, 2014). They are the

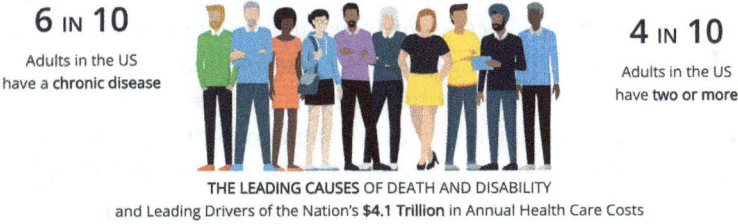

6 IN 10
Adults in the US
have a **chronic disease**

4 IN 10
Adults in the US
have **two or more**

THE LEADING CAUSES OF DEATH AND DISABILITY
and Leading Drivers of the Nation's **$4.1 Trillion** in Annual Health Care Costs

FIGURE 11   The leading causes of death and disability (Source: Centers for Disease Control and Prevention, https://www.cdc.gov/chronicdisease/resources/infographic/chronic-diseases.htm, Public domain)

leading cause of death and disability in the U.S., with heart disease being the leading contributor. These statistics add up to a $4.1 trillion health care cost (Centers for Disease Control and Prevention, Health and Economic Costs of Chronic Diseases, n.d.), with an estimate by the Centers for Medicare and Medicaid Services expecting that number to rise to $6 trillion by 2027.

Chronic diseases are a burden not only for patients experiencing ailments but also for their loved ones, who often must bridge the gaps that exist in strained healthcare systems. I remember being shaken by this awareness after my daughter's diabetes diagnosis. Rushing around one morning to weigh food and count carbs for my daughter's lunch so she could adequately calculate her insulin needs, my younger daughter quietly and calmly said, "You love Electra more." She was not angry, but recognizing the times I had said to my other kids – "hold on, I need to give Electra a shot" or "Wait a minute – I need to figure out how many carbs are in tonight's dinner," was a wake-up call. Until that moment, I had not realized how many times I had asked my other children to wait as I tried to walk the line that diabetes had drawn in the sand of our lives.

Waiting is another complication experienced by people managing chronic diseases. Studies in the United States have revealed an essential insight into how much time people spend waiting – for appointments, insurance and paychecks, prescriptions, and transportation to get them to healthcare clinics and pharmacies. The duration of waiting varies and is frequently tied to financial stability. Those who do not have insurance and rely on state and federal support have many additional hurdles to jump to qualify for assistance, a time-consuming process. While these individuals wait, their health concerns do not vanish (Lee et al., 2020).

Diabetes is a specific and unforgiving disease that requires a sense of urgency, especially type 1 diabetes; this is particularly relevant to those managing diabetes behind prison walls. Diagnosed two weeks before her tenth birthday, I cannot unhear my daughter's plea to not have diabetes for her birthday. Nevertheless, fifteen years later, she is thriving. I am confident that much of her ambition and success is due to our ability to effectively manage this persistent and incurable disease on a daily basis. This advantage is not the case for incarcerated individuals living with diabetes. Even when the necessary supplies are affordable, there are no days off when daily insulin injections are required to stay alive. Supreme Court Judge Sonia Sotomayor, who is living with diabetes, states that "when you have to treat a condition, you grow to be disciplined" (Stein, 2017, p. 4).

However, diabetes can be costly and exhausting. It is an insidious disease that can wear on one's pocketbook, perseverance, and resolve. Diabetes affects 34 million people in our country, or 10% of the population (American Diabetes Association, Statistics About Diabetes, n.d.). As an auto-immune disease, the chronic condition occurs when blood glucose levels are too high. Glucose comes from the food people eat, and the insulin that the body naturally produces allows glucose to enter cells that produce energy. Individuals with type 1 diabetes do not produce insulin and, therefore, must receive the hormone externally through injections or an insulin pump (Nichols, 2023). For those living with type 2 diabetes, the more common form of diabetes, the body may still produce some insulin, though typically not enough to convert the glucose and move it out of the bloodstream (Nichols, 2023). A standard blood test can

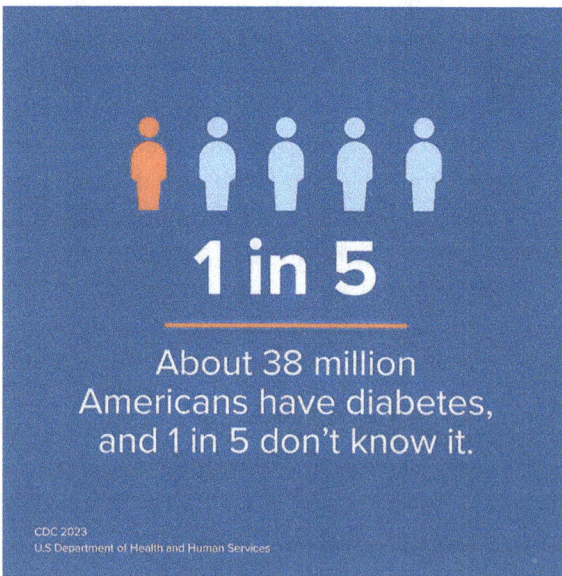

FIGURE 12   Diabetes in America (Source: Centers for Disease Control and Prevention. Diabetes Info Cards, https://www.cdc.gov/diabetes/library/socialmedia/infocards.html, Public domain)

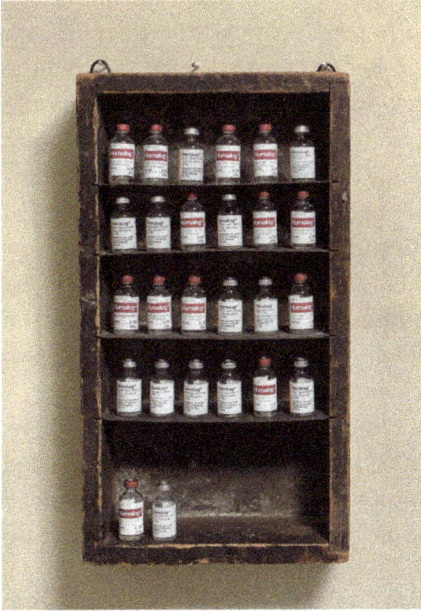

FIGURE 13
Twenty-Six (antique shelf with twenty-six
insulin bottles represents the age at which
young adults are removed from their parents'
insurance, often creating a precarious
circumstance)
PHOTOGRAPH: WHITE, 2020

reveal if a person has diabetes, and one type of assessment, an A1C test, can determine how well a person is managing their diabetes (Nichols, 2023). The lower the number, the better. Exercise and healthy meal choices can help control the disease. Nevertheless, for healthy management, an individual with diabetes should check blood glucose levels several times daily.

To effectively manage the disease, a person living with diabetes should always have several items on hand: insulin, blood glucose monitor, lancets, test strips, glucose tablets, syringes or an insulin pump, and a sharps container to secure used syringes and test strips. It is a deadly gamble to live without these necessary supplies, especially for someone living with type 1 diabetes. Health insurance is one of the most critical factors in ensuring that individuals have consistent care. However, this has proven a dangerous circumstance for young adults when they turn twenty-six years old and are no longer permitted to be on their parent's policies.

The Affordable Care Act was passed in 2010 and had many favorable attributes. One was allowing young adults to stay on their parent's health insurance policies until the age of twenty-six. The flip side is that the price of insulin skyrocketed in that time, leaving many scrambling to find their own insurance and trying to meet the growing price of copays for a lifesaving medication. Studies in the U.S. show that "millennials are far worse off financially than previous generations, with an average net worth below $8,000" (Hall, 2019, para. 5).

The focus of insulin was in the eye of a 2022 political storm before congressional Democrats passed the Inflation Reduction Act, which reduced the out-of-pocket cost of insulin. Republicans would go on to block a measure that would extend that price to those covered by private insurance (Luhby, 2023). In early 2023, the drugmaker Eli Lilly announced that it would follow the guidelines of the Inflation Redaction Act and cap the out-of-pocket costs at $35 a month for individuals with private insurance. Individuals without insurance can apply for assistance through Eli Lilly's copay assistance program. The drugmaker's announcement received praise from President Biden and the American Diabetes Association (Lovelace, Jr., 2023). The announcement also incentivized other makers of the drug to lower their prices.

President Biden later stepped in and, during his State of the Union Address, called for a cap on insulin pricing at $35 a month, for all Americans and called on other drugmakers to follow Eli Lilly's example. According to the American Diabetes Association, 8.4 million people in the United States are reliant on insulin produced by three makers – Eli Lilly, Novo Nordisk, and Sanofi. By March of 2023 both Sanofi and Novo Nordisk had announced their plan to follow Eli Lilly's lead (Luhby, 2023).

Since diabetes supplies can surpass $12,000 per year, there is a reckoning that those living with diabetes must face once they no longer have adequate health insurance. There is a loss of security, sufficient medical coverage, and, too often, a loss of life. Without access to insurance and the historically astronomical price of insulin, several young adults have died from diabetic ketoacidosis, also known as DKA. Unfortunately, it is not only young adults who experience this circumstance. Anyone living with diabetes is vulnerable to this complication. However, it most impacts those who struggle to quickly access necessary supplies, such as those who are incarcerated.

The physical ailments of chronic disease and illness are only one part of a patient's well-being. Mental health is a frequently overlooked component of chronic disease. Clinicians are trained to treat patients and the disease yet can oftentimes miss the importance of psychological health and well-being. This routine of psychological well-being is complex and includes personal, cognitive, communicative, and other non-psychological factors. The phenomenon of well-being is described as "a feeling of life satisfaction, quality of life, personal self-fulfillment, and creation of objective and subjective values" (Kudachi et al., 2023). The reality is that constant management of diabetes without a day off often leads to mental health stresses.

According to the Juvenile Diabetes Research Foundation, teens living with type 1 diabetes are five times more likely to have depression than their peers who do not have the disease (JDRF, n.d.).

In his book Life and Death on Rikers Island, the former chief medical officer for New York City's jails, Homer Venters, found neglect, sexual abuse, and
blocked access to care to be a regular occurrence. The story of one inmate,
Carlos Mercado, was featured in the book. Mercado died from diabetic ketoacidosis (DKA) after being denied insulin during the intake process after telling
the prison staff that he had diabetes (Venters, 2019, p. 15). Mercado's death highlights the way that incarceration poses an increased health risk for inmates.

> For a person to know that they are insulin-dependent – to report that and
> then for any state institution to fail to act on that, really puts the onus
> and responsibility for this man's death directly on the jail system. (Davies,
> 2019, para. 4)

The complication from diabetic ketoacidosis occurs when an individual's
body cannot produce insulin or does not receive insulin to allow blood sugar
to enter the cells for energy. Instead, the liver breaks down fat to use as fuel and
produces acids that are called ketones. When this happens quickly, it builds
up to dangerous levels in the body. Essentially, the body is poisoned by toxic
ketones (Centers for Disease Control, Diabetic Ketoacidosis, n.d.).

One mother described how her son died due to his inability to afford insulin
three days before his payday. "It shouldn't have happened. That cause of death
of diabetic ketoacidosis" (Sable-Smith, 2018, para. 3). The price of the life-saving
hormone has doubled since 2012 and put many people's lives in danger. For some
living with diabetes without insurance, the out-of-pocket expenses can cost
upward of $1300 per month. Some individuals fall into the gap between being
able to afford insurance and qualifying for government assistance or are faced
with a deductible that must first be met, an insurmountable obstacle for many.
This reality leads many people living with diabetes to ration their insulin supplies,
putting their lives in grave danger (Sable-Smith, 2018). According to the Centers
for Disease Control and Prevention, approximately 16.5% of people in the United
States who use insulin are rationing the drug due to its cost (Luhby, 2023).

A diagnosis of diabetes was a death sentence a century ago. In 1923, the
researchers Frederick Banting, Charles Best, and J.J.R. Macleod discovered a
method of extracting and purifying insulin that would become life-changing
for many. The patent for the discovery was then sold to the University of Toronto
for one dollar, with the goal of the life-saving hormone becoming available to
anyone who needed it. Recently, until 2022, one vial of insulin can cost approximately $250, with most patients requiring up to four vials per month. There
are varying opinions as to why the prices have soared, yet activists blame the
manufacturers of the drug (Sable-Smith, 2018).

The American Diabetes Association reports that individuals diagnosed with diabetes incurred over sixteen thousand dollars' worth of medical expenses, of which close to ten thousand was attributed directly to diabetes. Furthermore, those who are living with diabetes average 2.3 higher expenses for medical purposes than those without diabetes. In March of 2022, the United States House of Representatives passed a bill, The Affordable Insulin Now Act, to cap monthly insulin costs at $35 for insured patients, however this bill does not assist those without insurance. Within the United States, communities of color, Black, and Indigenous individuals are disproportionately living without adequate health insurance. Without other forms of assistance, such as MediCal or Medicaid, insulin costs can leave people having to "make impossible choices between covering different basic needs" or securing life-saving medications, such as insulin (McConnell, February 2022).

In addition to kids who age off their parent's insurance policies, other communities are especially vulnerable to a chronic disease diagnosis such as diabetes. Undocumented immigrants are one particular group who are four times more likely to be uninsured than those with citizenship. Given that these individuals must pay out of pocket for insulin, frequently, "they will pay for as much as they can afford and hope not to die" (McConnell, April 2022, para. 29). Furthermore, those who are financially compromised must pay a higher percentage of their overall income to meet their medical needs, which then disproportionately impacts quality of life needs such as food, rent, and the ability to have secure living conditions (McConnell, April 2022). The incarcerated community is another population that is particularly vulnerable to the costs and access to diabetic supplies necessary to their survival.

Public assistance such as Medicaid is available to some people who qualify, yet many, despite their low income, ironically make too much to qualify. In the United States, to be eligible for Medicaid, a single person without dependents would have to earn less than $17,774 yearly in most states to qualify. As of 2023, 10 states in the U.S. declined to adopt the 2010 Affordable Care Act, and therefore no single person without dependents is eligible for assistance. More than two million uninsured adults fall into the gap of making too much for government assistance yet not enough to be able to afford private insurance. Undocumented individuals, Black, and Indigenous communities are significantly impacted and fall into this divide (McConnell, April 2022).

Those who are incarcerated and living with diabetes face an especially dire challenge as they cannot readily access their needed supplies since "They are not allowed insulin injections, nor self-monitoring of blood sugar. They are not allowed to have any type of needle that could be considered a weapon in their jail cell" (Almekinder, 2018, para. 13). Unfortunately, few prisons employ

FIGURE 14
Time turned awry (time can feel elusive
when incarcerated, with individuals
frequently losing track of minutes, hours,
and days)
PHOTOGRAPH: WHITE, 2020

trained nurses. The staff is not appropriately qualified to provide diabetes care. "This is a big problem for Type 1 diabetics, as they frequently need four or more injections of insulin per day to get decent control" (Almekinder, 2018, para. 11).

Monique K., who has type 1 diabetes and was incarcerated in both California prisons and jails, received her insulin twice daily while having few problems with the guards. "I didn't give any problems, so they rarely gave me any. I was given my medication and checked on, so I can't complain" (K. Monique, personal communication, 2020). Yet she explained that the most challenging aspect of living with diabetes while incarcerated was feeling uncomfortable with someone controlling her medication.

The food options within prisons are another consideration that significantly contributes to compromised health outcomes for those with diabetes. Audra K, a formerly incarcerated woman in California, described the dilemma of inmates who wanted to eat healthier, yet it is nearly impossible without resources. For a person who does not have the financial means to shop the prison store for healthier food options, "you're screwed. You're hungry. You're going to eat what they give you, even though it's bad for you. And that's not right" (K. Audra, personal communication, 2020). The jobs offered within prisons typically pay between thirteen and fifty-two cents per hour, leaving little money for food (Carns & Weaver, 2022). Those with extra money from family support can purchase stolen food or extra snacks from the commissary when available, allowing for more nutritional options. However, this is often not possible for the incarcerated.

The provided food within prison walls lacks proper nutrition, contributing to existing health conditions like diabetes. According to the ACLU, sixty-two percent of formerly incarcerated individuals reported rarely having access to fresh produce. In contrast, the typical diet served within correctional facilities includes items "high in salt, sugar, and refined carbohydrates" (Carns & Weaver, 2022, para. 3), contributing to elevated rates of diabetes, hypertension, and high blood sugar.

A lack of care for incarcerated populations impacts society due to expensive medical care for formerly incarcerated individuals. Reentry and rehabilitation after incarceration is a feat, but poor health creates another hurdle to having a stable environment. One individual who was interviewed by the ACLU stated that he tried to create his own meals with commissary foods because the meals offered by the prison were harmful to his diabetes management (Carns & Weaver, 2022).

Part of the National Prison Project's litigation against U.S. prisons, jails, and detention centers focuses on health and nutrition for quality health care and humane conditions. Their view is that "aside from their constitutional right to the basic necessity of palatable and nutritious food, incarcerated people should be treated with dignity – and that includes a nutritious and healthful diet" (Carns & Weaver, 2022, para. 12).

Despite having health clinics within prison walls, individuals must jump many hurdles to access care. Many states charge individuals up to five dollars for a copay per doctor visit despite earning cents on the dollar for prison jobs. As of 2022, forty states require that copays are deducted from an individual's commissary fund. For many, the inability to pay these fees forces them to forgo seeing a medical provider for preventative care that can, in turn, become life-threatening and expensive (Kamin, 2022). Furthermore, the state cannot refuse an incarcerated person medical care. If an urgent situation arises, the copay is either automatically deducted from their commissary account or billed and paid with any future earnings or money they receive (Kamin, 2022).

On September 10, 2019, the California senate voted to pass Assembly Bill 45, eliminating copays for medical and dental treatment in California's correctional facilities. The legislation finally went into effect in early 2020, removing the $3 fee that prisoners must pay for treatment. A former prisoner, who is now a community organizer with the California Coalition for Women, commented that she earned eight cents per hour working in the prison kitchen, "but was still required to pay a fee to the doctor" (Marks, 2020, para. 4). She often chose to purchase soap instead of seeing a doctor when she needed medical care. This dilemma is consistent with the choices made by the individuals with whom I spoke. This choice can be detrimental for incarcerated people living with a dangerous and chronic illness, like diabetes.

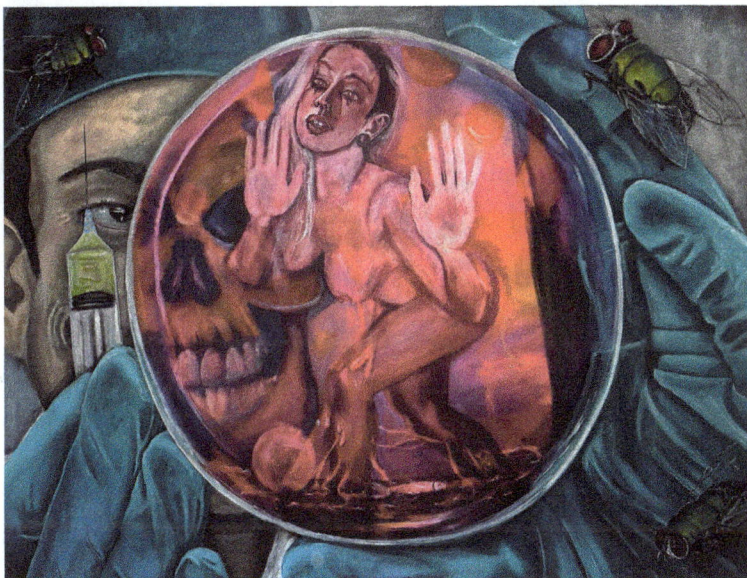

FIGURE 15   A fragile specimen
            PAINTING: ZEPH VONDENHUEVEL

Regarding incarcerated women and diabetes, T explained that she felt the guards used access to medication as a form of control and manipulation. Inmates are at the mercy of correctional officers for gaining access to their medications, therefore if a problem arises with the doctors or other prison personnel, the guards were trained to look the other way and not question protocol (T., personal communication, June 12, 2020). According to a former corrections nurse, the lack of education of officers working in a bad environment agitates an already precarious environment. There is a need to follow other countries, such as Norway, which require advanced training programs that take years vs. weeks to complete (Anonymous, personal communication, December 29, 2022).

The health outcomes for correctional officers are also very bad. The carceral environment is substandard for both guards and those who are incarcerated, and there are no support services for guards or prison staff (Anonymous, personal communication, 2023). One such program, AMEND at UCSF, founded by Brie Williams, M.D., aims to reduce the debilitating impacts on health for prison residents and the staff around them. AMEND's team also works with policymakers and community leaders to "advance decarceration strategies and a better, new system of accountability and healing in the U.S." (AMEND, 2023).

Incarceration in and of itself is a social condition and political problem that severely impacts health outcomes for correctional officers and incarcerated communities. Research has revealed that death by suicide among correctional

FIGURE 16   *Adrenaline exhale* (prison personnel are also at risk for health complications due to on-the-job stress)
PAINTING: DANIEL SUNDAHL

workers is more than seven times higher than among the general population in the United States (Ricciardelli et al., 2022). In addition to suicide, correctional staff stress levels lead to higher divorce rates, PTSD, and depression. Interacting with incarcerated populations daily and in a stressful workplace environment undermines officers' confidence and resilience and their inability to cope.

The build-up of circumstances on the job leads to consequences of critical stress, which in turn affects an officer's commitment to the job and therefore creates compassion fatigue (Chamberlain & Hompe, 2020). Compassion fatigue contributes to burnout and a lack of empathy toward those they are monitoring and caring for. Another formerly incarcerated Alabama resident spoke of the influence that correctional officers have in blocking access to health care. He commented that "the guards will block you from getting health care, and that it's a form of 'man leave me alone, I don't feel like being bothered.' They don't want to deal with it" (L.T., personal communication, June 14, 2022).

Meanwhile, there is a stereotype of incarcerated individuals as strong, scrappy, and agile. This personification was reinforced in 2011 by Justice Anthony Scalia in his dissent to the Supreme Court's Brown v. Plata decision. Filed on behalf of mentally and physically ill people who were incarcerated in California's overcrowded prisons, Scalia believed that those released as a result

of the case would not be individuals living with an illness but rather "fine physical specimens who have developed intimidating muscles pumping iron in the
prison gym" (Crane & Pascoe, 2020, para. 1).

Yet the reality is that incarceration both creates and exacerbates health
conditions. Evidence has shown an "increasingly elderly, overweight, and
chronically ill" (Crane & Pascoe, 2020, para. 2) population as research reflects
incarceration's negative impact on health for those imprisoned and their family members. Little data exists on the health complications resulting from
imprisonment as this issue is overlooked in most national health surveys. Yet
a 2011–12 survey revealed that forty percent of those detained in United States
jails and prisons suffer at least one chronic medical condition and experienced
increases in high blood pressure and diabetes, with rates of diabetes doubling
since 2004 (Crane & Pascoe, 2020). The U.S. Centers for Disease Control and
Prevention (CDC) estimates that eliminating three risk factors – poor diet,
inactivity, and smoking – would prevent 80% of heart disease and stroke, 80%
of type 2 diabetes, and 40% of cancer. Yet, these factors are ubiquitous for
many incarcerated individuals.

According to the Prison Policy Center, incarcerated individuals often have
similar rates of certain chronic conditions as the U.S. general population.
However, inadequate screening during intake and throughout a person's sentence can lead to undiagnosed conditions, leading to skewered statistics that
overlook likely health problems amongst the prison population (Wang, 2022).
Furthermore, the rate of incarceration for those over age 55 has increased five-
fold since 1990, and "the Census estimated a 4,440% increase in the number
of people in prison over age 55 between 1981 and 2030" due to both long-term
sentences and tough-on-crime policies (Crane & Pascoe, 2020, para. 15).

The incarcerated population has overall poorer health than non-incarcerated individuals, yet older detainees are especially in worse health than their
younger counterparts and have fewer visitors and familial support. Despite
the increasing rates of the aging prison demography, very little focus has been
placed on death and dying within prison walls. LaDarrius Dees, formerly incarcerated in Alabama's state prison, commented on seeing older men around
him dying within prison walls,

> Man, you got folks in behind walls, they sick. You got folks 60, 70, 80 years
> old who be doing 30, 40 years. These folks old now. They did enough time.
> Let them out. What can they do? They can barely walk. They can barely
> talk. Let them out so their family can take care of them. Those folks in
> prison are dying. (Dees, personal communication, 2022, June 14)

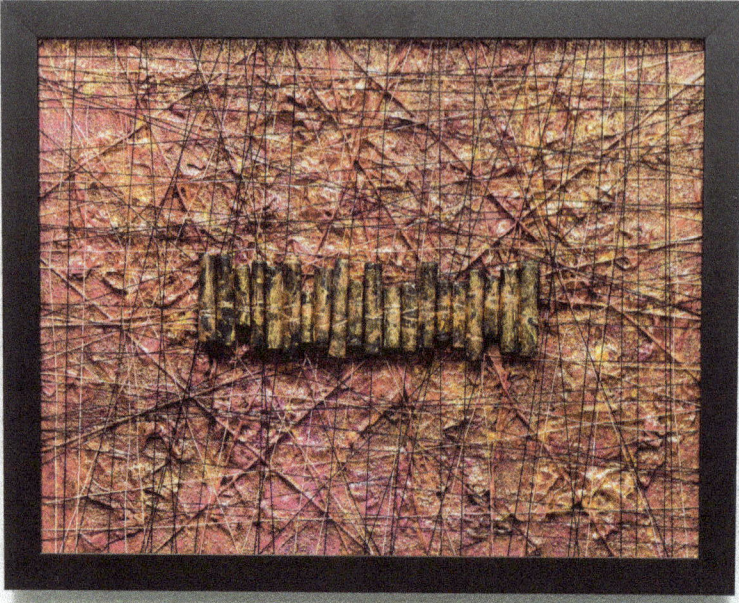

FIGURE 17   Mixed media (rolled cardboard, acrylic, and fibers on canvas panel. The image
reflects the overcrowding that occurs within the American prison system)
IMAGE: JOY HOOP

While the numbers for chronic health problems among the general population are consistent with those of incarcerated populations, correction facilities are not equipped to adequately care for those with extreme conditions (American Academy of Family Physicians, n.d.). Overcrowding and violence are significant factors in the vulnerability of incarcerated populations living with chronic illnesses. Overcrowded prisons continue to be a dangerous factor in the U.S., with the majority of states "operating at 75% or more of their capacity" (Prison Policy Initiative, n.d.) while nine state prisons and the federal Bureau of Prisons are operating at more than 100% of their capacity (Prison Policy Initiative, n.d.).

Overcrowding leads to many problems for both those incarcerated and for prison staff. Unsanitary conditions and violence are the two leading factors. An anonymous source who has worked in both men's and women's prisons in the Midwest commented,

Individuals think the medical staff does not care, yet medical personnel have their hands tied due to admin rules. As a nurse, you are trained to care and to have a therapeutic relationship. While establishing any kind of therapeutic relationship inside the prison goes against security. And you're constantly in battle with what security wants and what adequate care is and should be.

Overcrowding takes away from the time you can focus on individuals and their health concerns (Anonymous, personal communication, 2023).

While prison communities are entitled to health care, no mandate on the quality and consistency of care is needed. Most prison medical facilities need to be more staffed for overcrowded facilities. This circumstance was a reality that most people in society were unaware of until the COVID-19 pandemic in 2020 severely impacted jails and prisons across the nation. Nevertheless, there continues to be a need for education and awareness around the industrial prison complex in the United States and its impact on health outcomes in and outside correctional facilities.

Utilizing art and visual representations about health care and incarceration is an effective way to bring forth information to those not directly impacted by incarceration. Visual representation occurs in a variety of methods. According to B.D. Roe and E.P Ross, in their book, The Language Arts, include images and visual representations of photographs, drawings, and diagrams, in addition to video presentations and dioramas (Roe & Ross, n.d.). The six language arts that the authors discuss include:

- Listening: understanding spoken language
- Speaking: communicating ideas through oral language
- Reading: understanding written language
- Writing: communicating through written language
- Viewing: understanding visual images and connecting them to accompany-ing spoken or written words
- Visually representing: presenting information through pictures, either alone or along with spoken or written words

A visual message can resonate with a viewer and provide a more precise understanding, including emotional persuasiveness and impact in the mate-rials. "Visuals are thought to send people along emotive pathways where tex-tual/verbal material leaves them in a more rational, logical, and linear pathway of thought" (Joffe, 2008, p. 84). Researchers Aarti Iyer and Julian Oldmeadow found that in the case of a news story focusing on a kidnapped journalist, the audience felt significantly more fearful when the story was visually told than those who had only read about it. Those who saw the images were "engaged and concerned" and "stirred by the visuals" (Joffe, 2008, p. 85).

Furthermore, activist art and visual representations allow incarcerated indi-viduals to express their journey, especially for those with limited educational and literacy levels. Infographics and visual representations of an experience, such as healthcare and incarceration, are valuable means of providing "a format that utilizes engaging visuals that not only appeal to an audience hungry for information but also aid in the comprehension of and retention of that material" (Lankow et al., 2012, p. 12).

References

Almekinder, E. (2018, October 14). *Diabetes care in prison: How to manage your diabetes in prison.* TheDiabetesCouncil.com. https://www.thediabetescouncil.com/diabetes-care-in-prison-how-to-manage-your-diabetes-in-prison/

AMEND. (2023, November 2). *A public health approach to addressing prison harms.* https://amend.us/

American Diabetes Association (ADA). (n.d.). *Statistics about diabetes.* https://www.diabetes.org/resources/statistics/statistics-about-diabetes

American Academy of Family Physicians. (n.d.). *Poverty and health – The family medicine perspective* (Position Paper). https://www.aafp.org/about/policies/all/poverty-health.html

Bernell, S., & Howard, S. W. (2016). Choose your words carefully: What is a chronic disease? *Front Public Health, 4,* 159. https://www.ncbi.nlm.nih.gov/pmc/articles/PMC4969287/

Carns, J., & Weaver, S. (2022, November 23). Two cups of broth and rotting sandwiches: The reality of mealtime in prisons and jails. *ACLU News and Commentary.* https://www.aclu.org/news/prisoners-rights/the-reality-of-mealtime-in-prisons-and-jails

Chaffey, C. (2021). *30 Days to understanding chronic illness and pain.* Risen Books.

Centers for Disease Control and Prevention. (2024, May 15). *Diabetic ketoacidosis.* https://www.cdc.gov/diabetes/about/diabetic-ketoacidosis.html?CDC_AAref_Val=https://www.cdc.gov/diabetes/basics/diabetic-ketoacidosis.html

Centers for Disease Control and Prevention. (2024, July 12). *Health and economic costs of chronic diseases.* https://www.cdc.gov/chronic-disease/data-research/facts-stats/index.html

Centers for Medicare and Medicaid Services. (n.d.). *National health expenditure data fact sheet.* https://www.cms.gov/Research-Statistics-Data-and-Systems/Statistics-Trends-and-Reports/NationalHealthExpendData/NHE-Fact-Sheet

Chamberlain, M., & Hompe, B. (2020, June 22). *Causes of stress for correctional officers.* Lexipol. https://www.lexipol.com/resources/blog/causes-of-stress-for-correctional-officers/

Crane, J. T., & Pascoe, K. (2020, November 11). Becoming institutionalized: Incarceration as a chronic health condition. *Medical Anthropology Quarterly*. https://doi.org/10.1111/maq.12621

Davies, D. (2019, March 18). Former physician at Rikers Island exposes health risks of incarceration. *WBUR News*. Podcast. https://www.wbur.org/npr/704424675/former-physician-at-rikers-island-exposes-health-risks-of-incarceration

Edwards, L. (2014). *In the Kingdom of the sick: A social history of chronic illness in America*. Bloomsbury Publishing.

Hall, E. (2019, July 21). Turning 26 is a potential death sentence for people with type 1 diabetes in America. *BuzzFeed News*. https://www.buzzfeednews.com/article/ellievhall/turning-26-type-1-diabetes

JDRF. (n.d.). *Type 1 diabetes and depression*. https://www.jdrf.org/t1d-resources/living-with-t1d/mental-health/depression/

Joffe, H. (2008, February). The power of visual material: Persuasion, emotion, and identification. *Diogenes*. https://www.researchgate.net/publication/249742695_The_Power_of_Visual_Material_Persuasion_Emotion_and_Identification

Kamin, G. (2022, 18 September). Forty states still charge prisoners co-pays for medical care. *Observer*. https://observer.com/2022/09/forty-states-still-charge-prisoners-co-pays-for-medical-care/

Kudachi, A. B., Hogade, A. P., Koppard, S. R., Mudhol, R. S., & Javali, S. B. (2023, January–April). Correlation between psychological well-being of people with chronic diseases in executive health checkup. *Journal of the Scientific Society, 50*(1), 102–107.

Lankow, J., Ritchie, J., & Crooks, R. (2012). Infographics. The power of visual storytelling. *Column Five Media*. https://www.columnfivemedia.com/book/

Lee, A. A., James, A. S., & Hun, J. M. (2020, November). Waiting for care: Chronic illness and health system uncertainties in the United States. *Social Science and Medicine*. https://www.ncbi.nlm.nih.gov/pmc/articles/PMC7435333/

Lovelace, B., Jr. (2023, 1 March). Drugmaker Eli Lilly caps the cost of insulin at $35 a month, bringing relief for millions. *NBC Health News*. https://www.nbcnews.com/health/health-news/eli-lilly-caps-cost-insulin-35-month-rcna72713

Luhby, T. (2023, March 16). Sanofi becomes latest drugmaker to announce insulin price cuts, capping cost at $35 for the privately insured. *CNN Health*. https://www.cnn.com/2023/03/16/health/sanofi-insulin-price-reduction/index.html

Marks, C. (2020, January, 9). Prisoner co-payments for health care services eliminated in California. *Prison Legal News*. https://www.prisonlegalnews.org/news/2020/jan/9/prisoner-co-payments-health-care-services-eliminated-california/

Martin, C. M. (2007, December). Chronic disease and illness care. *Canadian Family Physician, v. 53*(12). https://www.ncbi.nlm.nih.gov/pmc/articles/PMC2231531/

McConnell, M. (2022, April 14). "If I'm Out of Insulin, I'm Going to Die." *Human Rights Watch*. https://www.hrw.org/report/2022/04/12/if-im-out-insulin-im-going-die/united-states-lack-regulation-fuels-crisis

Nichols, H. (2023, December 18). Diabetes. The differences between types 1 and 2. *Medical News Today*. https://www.medicalnewstoday.com/articles/7504.php

Reynolds, R., Dennis, S., Hasan, I., Slewa, J., Chen, W., Tian, D., & Zwar, N. (2018). A systematic review of chronic disease management interventions in primary care. *BMC Family Practice, 19*, Article number: 11. https://bmcprimcare.biomedcentral.com/articles/10.1186/s12875-017-0692-3

Ricciardelli, R., McKendy, L., Laleh, J., & Carleton, R. N. (2022, June). Mental health disorders and suicide behaviors among provincial correctional workers. *Journal of Occupational and Environmental Medicine, 64*(6), 504–509. https://journals.lww.com/joem/fulltext/2022/06000/mental_health_disorders_and_suicidal_behaviors.9.aspx

Roe, B. P., & Ross, E. P. (n.d.). *The language arts*. Pearson Allyn Bacon Prentice Hall. https://www.dr-hatfield.com/EDUC536/docs/The6LanguageArts.pdf

Sable-Smith, B. (2018, September 1). Insulin's high cost leads to lethal rationing. *NPR*. https://www.npr.org/sections/health-shots/2018/09/01/641615877/insulins-high-cost-leads-to-lethal-rationing

Salib, V. (2022). Chronic disease rates and management strain the US Healthcare System. *Life Sciences Intelligence*. https://lifesciencesintelligence.com/features/chronic-disease-rates-and-management-strain-the-us-healthcare-system

Stein, R. (2017). The 2016 Stein lecture: A conversation between U.S. Supreme Court justice Sonia Sotomayor and Professor Robert A. Stein. https://scholarship.law.umn.edu/cgi/viewcontent.cgi?article=1658&context=faculty_articles

Wang, L. (2022, June). Chronic punishment: The unmet health needs of people in state prisons. *Prison Policy Initiative*. https://www.prisonpolicy.org/reports/chronicpunishment.html

Venters, H. (2019). *Life and death on Rikers Island*. John Hopkins University Press.

The COVID-19 Pandemic

> This pandemic has magnified every existing inequality in our society
> – like systemic racism, gender inequality, and poverty.
> MELINDA GATES

∴

The stories started in early January 2020. A virus was sweeping through China, with a few cases in the U.S. My ex-husband, who suffered from comorbidities, packed up himself and my youngest daughter and headed for his expansive ranch in Northern California. I thought he was overreacting. I boarded a flight to New York, rolling my eyes at his panicked reaction. While on the East Coast, I was cautious yet, in hindsight, careless. I attended meetings and, on what would be the last night of Broadway shows before going dark, saw a production inside a packed, unmasked theater. I joked with friends in attendance about how lucky we were not to be fatalists running for the hills. We were wrong. And, we were lucky.

After a week on the East Coast, I returned to California. The next day, Governor Newsom put California into lockdown. At first, the rigid restrictions allowed a reprieve from my typically frenetic schedule. Too quickly, however, I felt unsettled, restless, and frustrated. I can only now look back at this naive and entitled viewpoint – I was safe and healthy. I had options that many did not. Those who were financially and medically compromised, and the thousands of incarcerated individuals locked into small spaces with no possibility of following CDC guidelines for social distancing did not enjoy the same privileges while navigating through the COVID-19 pandemic.

The COVID-19 pandemic of 2020 had a colossal impact on how people lived while adapting to a new and frightening reality. Not only did communities have to move differently worldwide, but they also had to adapt to remote working and learning. Schools, businesses, and individuals used videoconferencing to conduct classes, meetings, and socially distanced visits. Safety and convenience were the driving factors when shelter-in-place orders were first implemented. However, many new social media and videoconferencing users grew to appreciate visual outreach's benefits. "The visualization of information is enabling us insight and understanding quickly and efficiently, utilizing the incredible processing power of the human visual system" (Lankow et al., 2012, p. 12).

These new protocols and ways of staying connected worked well for the general public during the pandemic. However, those behind bars were restricted from having family visits, and access to phone calls was minimal due to the risk of contamination between individuals. Even in non-pandemic times, incarceration can feel incredibly isolating. After visitations ceased, most people did not get to see or hug their children and loved ones for over two years. An incarcerated mother in California admitted, "I feel that my kids maybe even feel like I abandoned them because, you know, how am I going to explain to the 5- and 6-year-old that they can't see me?" (Bryant, 2022, para. 2).

As the parent of a child with an autoimmune disease, my fears of being unable to protect her and make her less vulnerable resurfaced during the pandemic. She lived alone with only in-person contact during this time with her boyfriend, whom I was immensely grateful for. Zoom calls replaced our family dinners, yet it allowed us to see each other and have some sense of connection. It was not the same as in person, but it was something. Unlike families with relatives and loved ones living behind bars, I knew my daughter, while more at risk than some, was safe.

Prisons and jails are crowded spaces. Even when facilities operate under capacity, hundreds of individuals are housed in close contact units with limited social distancing. Add to this a population with challenging health concerns and limited medical staff to address the numerous and vastly different conditions. As discussed in Chapter 1, incarceration is a social determinant of health that creates and worsens health outcomes. Not surprisingly, jail and prison populations were quickly overcome with the virus when the COVID-19 pandemic swept the world in 2020.

Incarcerated populations were five times more likely than the general public to test positive for the COVID virus (Peterson & Brinkley-Rubenstein, 2021), and the COVID death rate was twenty percent higher for carceral populations (USA Facts, 2023). By early 2021, only ten states had vaccinated more than seventy percent of their incarcerated populations, creating locked-down epicenters of the virus inside prison walls. In addition to not receiving vaccination shots, the mortality rate for incarcerated people increased due to higher rates of chronic illnesses, stress, and the inability to socially distance (Herring & Widra, 2021).

The lack of humanity within correctional facilities during the COVID-19 pandemic revealed how incarcerated individuals are treated daily. As of early 2023, close to three thousand imprisoned people have died of the virus, with another

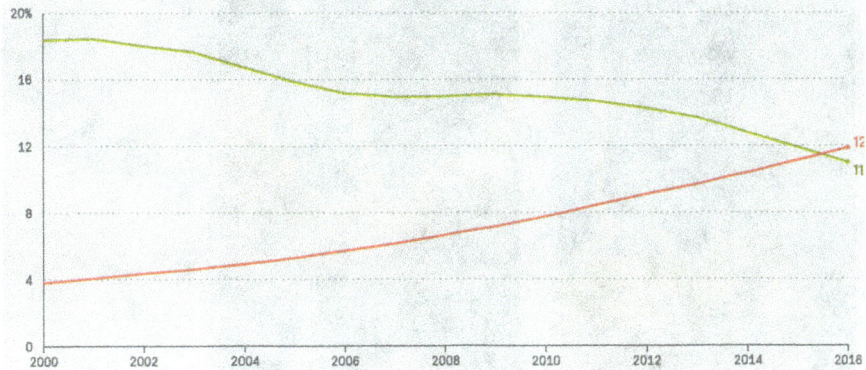

FIGURE 18   Percentage of incarcerated people over the age of 55 between 2000 and 2016
(the percentage of incarcerated people over the age of 55 [shown in orange]
has consistently increased in contrast to a decrease in those aged 18–24 [shown in
green]) (Source: The Marshall Project)

645,000 infected (COVID Prison Project, n.d.). Eighty-three percent of U.S. state
and federal prison deaths were individuals over fifty-five (Carson et al., 2022).
These statistics are profound given that, for the first time, older adults make up
a large share of state prison inmates, in addition to the eleven percent of the
federal prison population over fifty-six years old (Li & Lewis, 2020).

The growing populace of aging incarcerated adults stems from the tough-
on-crime and three-strikes laws established in the 1980s and 90s, of which
many of these individuals came from disenfranchised communities of color.
Furthermore, the incarcerated community of seniors faced the risk of their age
and pre-existing chronic health complications. Poorly equipped correctional
medical facilities to treat those in dire need are even more dangerous to those
with chronic health needs.

Researchers have found that this growing population faces chronic health
problems "such as hypertension and diabetes, and they're more likely to
have limited mobility and increased mental health issues" (Li & Lewis, 2020,
para. 11). Added stress and a lack of quality medical options ages these individuals faster than those in the general population, who typically suffer from these
same issues at a much older age. Scientists believe that a weakened immune
system for seniors due to health complications is the reason for the increased
COVID-19 death rate for this age bracket (Li & Lewis. 2020).

The formerly incarcerated artist Kenneth Webb utilized his artistic abili-
ties with supplies available to him to process his experience of living through
the COVID-19 pandemic, while incarcerated, in his 2020 rocket diptych by

FIGURE 19   Painting by Kenneth Webb (2020. "The rocket pieces are about prison and what
                   the moment felt like, watching those that have the ability to leave, leave prison
                   during COVID-19.")
                   PHOTOGRAPH: JEFF MCLANE

illustrating the experience of those incarcerated at the beginning of the
pandemic.

In early 2020, medical experts provided a COVID-19 survival guide for incarcerated populations. However, the lack of access to prison computer screens
and the autonomy to follow their recommendations could have been more
secure, at best. The experts recognized that those detained within correctional
facilities did not have the same supplies and space as those outside. Instead,
they provided prison and jail adaptations such as ensuring that hand sanitizer
had at least 60 percent alcohol, filling bottles in the shower that could later
be heated up and used for hand washing, washing up with soap and water in
individual cells rather than taking a communal shower, and when outside of
the cell, covering up mouth and nose with t-shirts, a do-rag, or for women,
repurposing headscarves and bras into masks. Though not ideal, these solutions provided resourceful alternatives. Furthermore, the team recommended
that individuals try to purchase rubber gloves from the commissary and use
bed sheets on open bar cells to reduce exposure to nighttime coughing and
sneezing if allowed by correctional staff (Bartley et al., 2020).

The protocols and living arrangements within correctional facilities were not amendable to a pandemic and the need for social distancing. As described by Jennifer Graves, incarcerated at the Florida Women's Reception Center, the open dorm where she sleeps has "78 beds, eight showers, 12 toilets, and eight sinks. Our bunks are only 2 feet apart, side by side" (Lewis, n.d.). Many individuals were placed into solitary confinement to quarantine. Under normal circumstances, this would be a harsh and traumatic punishment, now being used as a protectant against the virus. Yet solitary confinement has a profound impact on a person's mental health. The alternative to "the hole," as solitary confinement is frequently called, is an 8x12 foot cell with only a bunk bed and one other person and very little access to fresh air, showers, or the ability to call or email family (Lewis, n.d.).

Fortunately, the Department of Corrections in several states decided to provide early release for low-risk individuals. Between January 2020 and February 2021, the State Department of Corrections and the Bureau of Prisons released 648,000 people from prison, and approximately six percent of those were listed as expedited releases. An expedited release is classified as an early release from their "expected release date or date of eligibility for post-custody supervision in the community" (Carson et al., 2022).

The wardens at federal prisons were more stringent and less compassionate with early releases. Nearly eleven thousand individuals in federal prisons requested a compassionate release between March and May 2020, yet only 156 of those applications were granted. At federal prisons in Texas and Louisiana, the wardens did not review or respond to the submitted requests. Some individuals chose to take the bureau to court to overturn a warden's decision, while others became victims of the virus. By 2022, 134 federal prisoners had died of the COVID-19 virus, while more than fifteen thousand tested positive (Neff & Blakinger, 2020).

One example of this decision-making is reflected in the story of Marie Neba, who was incarcerated in North Texas for Medicare fraud. In 2021, the fifty-six-year-old wrote about her stage-4 cancer diagnosis and how she struggled to walk due to body pain and foot numbness from her chemotherapy sessions. She explained that "the way things are going regarding my treatments here at Carswell can lead me to my grave" (Neff & Blakinger, 2020, para. 1). Despite having three children waiting to care for her at home, Neba's request for a compassionate release was denied. She tried again for a compassionate release after the COVID pandemic swept through the prison and was denied again. Neba was one of six women at the Carswell prison who died during the pandemic (Neff & Blakinger, 2020).

The warden of Elkton Prison in Ohio denied 866 out of the 867 compassionate release requests he received between March and May 2020, despite more

In the first three months of the COVID-19 pandemic, more than 10,000 federal prisoners **applied** for compassionate release. Wardens **denied** or **did not respond** to almost all of those requests, **approving only 156.**

From March through May, **10,940** federal prisoners applied for compassionate release.

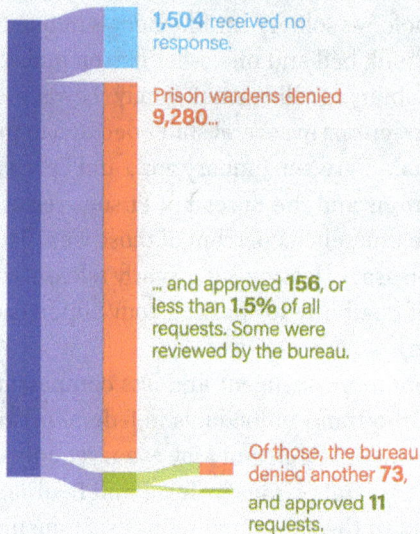

1,504 received no response.

Prison wardens denied **9,280...**

... and approved **156**, or less than **1.5%** of all requests. Some were reviewed by the bureau.

Of those, the bureau denied another **73**, and approved **11** requests.

FIGURE 20
Compassionate release statistics (Bureau of Prisons approved less than 1% of compassionate release requests) (Source: The Marshall Project)

than nine hundred individuals getting sick and nine COVID fatalities. Over 690 people tested positive for the virus at the Terminal Island prison in California, yet only five out of the 256 compassionate release requests were granted. Several prisons had a meager number of compassionate release requisitions, which prompted the American Civil Liberties Union (ACLU) to believe that record-keeping errors were happening. According to Somil Trivedi, an ACLU senior staff attorney, "I just don't feel like they're counting all of them. This has to be an undercount because of the informal nature of the process" (Neff & Blakinger, 2020, para. 21).

The 1600 compassionate releases that were approved were initiated by the person making the request, either on their own or with the help of an attorney. However, there were many cases that prison officials believed deserved a release. Yet, it is rare for the Bureau of Prisons officials to initiate the request, so much so that defense attorneys refer to this practice as unicorns. Los Angeles senior federal defender Davina Chen stated, "We are not aware of a single BOP-initiated motion for compassionate release based on the heightened risk of severe illness from COVID-19 infection" (Neff & Blakinger, 2020, para. 34).

Another aspect of the COVID lockdown was a shift in food service and routines for those behind bars. At the beginning of the pandemic, the jails in Orange County, California, halted hot food service within their jails. People were instead served sack lunches that were not always safe to consume due to rotting bologna and the highly processed options, which is detrimental for those with high blood pressure, diabetes, and heart problems. This practice continued for two years in some facilities, leading the American Civil Liberties Union to file a lawsuit on behalf of those affected, believing that "it is not only inhumane but an issue of public health" (Carns & Weaver, 2022, para. 9).

Another facility in Boston, Massachusetts, was found to provide inadequate food to sick and pregnant individuals in the medical infirmary. One man treated for a broken jaw received only two cups of broth for every meal. In contrast, a 17-week pregnant woman discussed having hunger pains and being told she was getting small portions because she was not burning enough calories with outdoor activities. Incarcerated populations have a constitutional right to health care and nutritious food. They also have a right to be treated with dignity, "and that includes a nutritious and healthful diet" (Carns & Weaver, 2022, para. 12).

Family members who had a loved one behind bars during the pandemic suffered their own trauma. Research revealed that seventy-nine percent of people with an incarcerated family member were highly distressed and concerned about their loved one contracting or potentially dying from the COVID-19 virus. Most of those who fell into this demographic were women with a child or spouse in the system. A Texas mother described how her son was locked in a cell for 23 hours per day while temperatures rose above a hundred degrees. She was concerned he would die from the conditions or his own doing. Another father felt that his son's living conditions were comparable "to a concentration camp" (Testa & Fahmy, 2021, para. 11).

Connecting with an incarcerated family member, especially a parent, is imperative for a healthy psychological connection. Researchers have found that consistent family visits lower recidivism rates and restore family connections. Children who experience the loss of a parent to incarceration suffer from decreased psychological, developmental, and financial health. As of 2022, more than five million children in the United States had experienced having a parent in prison or jail during their lifetime. Visitations and interpersonal touch vs. visitations through a glass barrier area are also positive benefits for children of incarcerated parents (Bryant, 2022).

FIGURE 21   COVID Masquerade by Diego Rios (Diego Rios is inspired by his Latin history, which includes Aztec and Mayan symbols. During the COVID-19 pandemic, the artist used his artistic skills to confront the pandemic's social and economic impacts and explore the death toll the virus was causing, Courtesy of the artist)

I've heard it said before that you never stop being a parent regardless of how old your children become. While I logically believed this, it was not until the COVID pandemic prevented me from having safe access to my daughter that I fully felt it. As a parent, we are meant to protect our children, to shelter them from harm and dangers. My anxiety over my lack of control was at odds with the reality that my daughter is a responsible adult who has a reliable partner who cares for and supports her. It is unfathomable to imagine what parents of incarcerated children or co-parents had to face. The inability to assist a vulnerable loved one is anxiety-inducing at its best and gut-wrenching at worst.

So how are things post-pandemic for those who remain incarcerated as the world begins to unfurl from this unprecedented phenomenon? The Prison

Policy Initiative studied the consequences of COVID-19 on incarcerated populations and explored what can be done to prevent the subsequent inevitable viral outbreak. A historic pattern reveals the vulnerability of individuals serving sentences in jails and prisons across the United States, as many "bear the disproportionate burden of public health crises, inevitably affecting the health of communities outside of correctional facilities as well" (Widra, April 2023, para. 3).

To prevent more illness and death within carceral facilities, protocols and procedures need to be addressed by correctional administrators and policymakers. Medical experts and correctional leaders must implement new strategies such as reducing overcrowding and lowering prison populations, improving health services, providing preventative support, developing systems that can quickly respond to virtual outbreaks, and providing immunizations and vaccines to those unable to quarantine and social distance themselves.

The mortality rate within U.S. prisons rose by sixty-one percent during the COVID-19 outbreak. There is a tremendous need for the Department of Corrections to reflect on and review past protocols to improve future health outcomes for both incarcerated populations and the staff working beside them (Widra, 2023). Visual representation through photography and artwork can highlight these statistics and encourage social activism to enact change. Artists like Diego Rios and many others used this format to comprehend their experiences and connect with others going through similar circumstances.

References

Bartley, L., Williams, B., & Rorvig, L. (2020, May 5). COVID-19: A survival guide for incarcerated people. *The Marshall Project.* https://www.themarshallproject.org/2020/05/05/covid-19-a-survival-guide-for-incarcerated-people

Bryant, E. (2022, May 19). *Two years of COVID-19 have fueled a crisis of isolation in prisons.* Vera Institute of Justice. https://www.vera.org/news/two-years-of-covid-19-have-fueled-a-crisis-of-isolation-in-prisons

Carns, J., & Weaver, S. (2022, November 23). Two cups of broth and rotting sandwiches: The reality of mealtime in prisons and jails. *ACLU News and Commentary.* https://www.aclu.org/news/prisoners-rights/the-reality-of-mealtime-in-prisons-and-jails

Carson, A. E., Nadel, M., & Gaes, G. (2022, August). *Impact of COVID-19 on state and federal prisons. March 2020–February 2021.* Special Report. U.S. Department of Justice Office of Justice Programs Bureau of Justice Statistics. https://bjs.ojp.gov/content/pub/pdf/icsfp2021.pdf

Herring, T., & Widra, E. (2021, May 18). Just over half of incarcerated people are vacci-
    nated, despite being locked in COVID-19 epicenters. *Prison Policy Initiative.*
    https://www.prisonpolicy.org/blog/2021/05/18/vaccinationrates/

Lankow, J., Ritchie, J., & Crooks, R. (2012). *Infographics: The power of visual storytelling.*
    Wiley.

Lewis, N. (n.d.). How we survived COVID-19 in prison. *The Marshall Project.*
    https://d63kb4t2ifcex.cloudfront.net/covidillustratednarrative/assets/how-we-
    survived-covid-19-in-prison.a9a40027.pdf

Li, W., & Lewis, N. (2020, March 19). This chart shows why the prison population is so
    vulnerable to COVID-19. *The Marshall Project.* https://www.themarshallproject.org/
    2020/03/19/this-chart-shows-why-the-prison-population-is-so-vulnerable-to-
    covid-19

Long, A. (2021, March 17). *Through cultures of constraint and care: The relentless art of
    Aimee Wissman.* Folklife.

Neff, J., & Blakinger, K. (2020, October 7). Thousands of sick Federal prisoners sought
    compassionate release. 98 Percent Were Denied. *The Marshall Project.*
    https://www.themarshallproject.org/2020/10/07/thousands-of-sick-federal-
    prisoners-sought-compassionate-release-98-percent-were-denied

Peterson, M., & Brinkley-Rubinstein, L. (2021, October 19). Incarceration is a health
    threat. Why isn't it monitored like one? *Health Affairs Forefront.*
    https://www.healthaffairs.org/content/forefront/incarceration-health-threat-
    why-isn-t-monitored-like-one

Testa, A., & Fahmy, C. (2021, April 20). No visits and barely any calls – pandemic makes
    separation even scarier for people with a family member in prison. *The Conversation.*
    https://theconversation.com/no-visits-and-barely-any-calls-pandemic-makes-
    separation-even-scarier-for-people-with-a-family-member-in-prison-158592

Third City Project, COVID Prison Project. (n.d.). https://3rdcityproject.com/index.php/
    data-dashboard-1/

USA Facts. (2023, July 23). *US COVID-19 cases and deaths by state.* https://usafacts.org/
    visualizations/coronavirus-covid-19-spread-map/

Widra, E. (2023, April 21). Lessons from COVID-19 can help prisons & jails prepare
    for the next pandemic. *Prison Policy Initiative.* https://www.prisonpolicy.org/blog/
    2023/04/21/pandemic-lessons-learned/

CHAPTER 4

Incarceration

> Prisons do not disappear social problems, they disappear human
> beings.
> ANGELA DAVIS

∵

I often think of Bryan Stevenson's quote, "Each one of us is more than the worst thing we've ever done." It elicits an inventory of things I have done in my life that may have drawn the attention of a police officer or pushed the limits of legality. Actions deemed innocuous – running a red light or smoking pot as a curious teenager – are actions that have put others behind bars. I consider myself fortunate that my race and small-town upbringing in a tight-knit community allowed me to avoid repercussions for my adolescent antics. However, many have not been so fortunate.

One out of every two adults in the United States has been impacted by incarceration and has had a family member in jail or prison. By 2020, more than 5 million people were under the supervision of the criminal justice system. Furthermore, researchers have estimated that approximately $182 billion is spent on staffing carceral institutions and supporting the more than 2 million incarcerated Americans and their families (Kuhn, 2021).

More than 600,000 individuals are released annually from American prisons, and nine million are in the local jail system. According to the National Institute of Justice, close to forty-four percent of those released will return to the criminal justice system within the first year. In 2005, an additional sixty-eight percent were re-arrested within three years for a new crime, while another seventy-seven percent were arrested within five years of release (World Population Review, n.d.).

Since the 1970s, the United States has ranked among the highest worldwide incarceration rates for the past fifty years, increasing by seven hundred percent between 1972 and 2009, outpacing most other countries (Ghandnoosh, 2021). While there has been a decline over the past ten years, much work remains. According to writer Nazgol Ghandnoosh, with the slight decrease in incarceration rates, it will take fifty-seven years to cut the current prison population

© TAMARA WHITE, 2025 | DOI:10.1163/9789004710610_005

FIGURE 22   We are all human[1]
PAINTING: WHITE, 2020

in half. Despite reduced rates of incarceration and lengths of sentences, some states, such as Alabama, are choosing to build more prisons due to overcrowding rather than following the lead of those making positive changes. Additionally, Montana, Idaho, Nebraska, and Kansas failed to reduce incarceration rates but also had the highest rates of prison populations in 2019 (Ghandnoosh, 2021).

The rise in incarceration began in the early 1970s during Richard Nixon's Presidency as he declared war on drugs and a movement to get tough on crime. That trend continued into Ronald Reagan's years in the White House, with the rate of incarceration doubling from 329,000 people detained in 1980 to 627,000 eight years later when he left office. Individuals of color were disproportionately incarcerated at rates far higher than White communities, then and now. While the overall rates of incarceration spanned across federal and state prisons, the majority of the increased numbers were under state facilities (Cullen, 2018).

In 1994, President Bill Clinton signed the Violent Crime Control and Law Enforcement Act into Congress, now called the 1994 crime bill. This single decision created a confusing and complicated law that incentivized states to

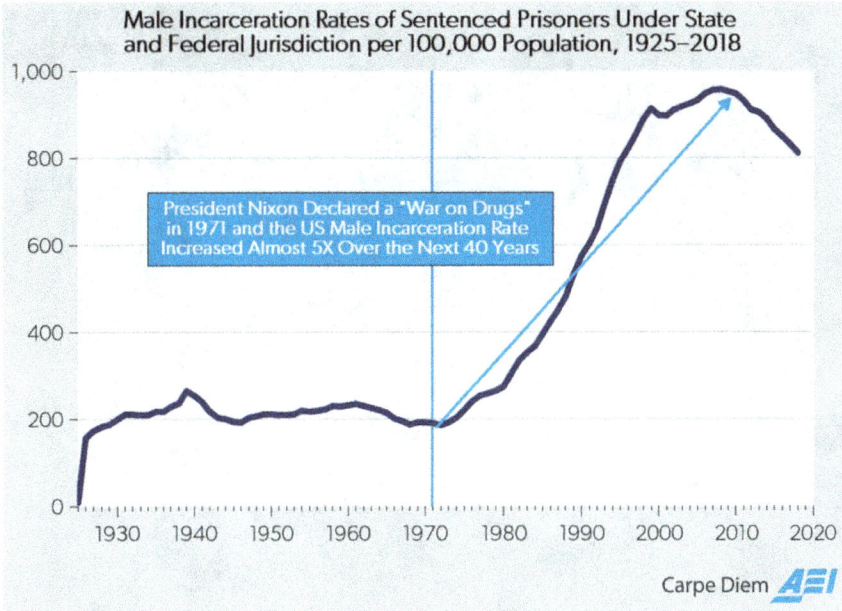

FIGURE 23   Male incarceration rates of sentenced prisoners under state and federal
            jurisdiction per 100,000 population, 1925–2018 (Source: https://www.aei.org/
            carpe-diem/the-shocking-story-behind-nixons-declaration-of-a-war-on-drugs-on-
            this-day-in-1971-that-targeted-blacks-and-anti-war-activists-3/)

incarcerate more people yet also protected women in abusive relationships
and victims through an assault weapons ban (Eisen, 2020). Furthermore, states
were encouraged to build more prisons and jails. This new law was the most
significant crime bill in United States history. However, there is minimal evidence that the public was safer due to the tough-on-crime approach (Chung
et al., 2019).

The 1994 law encouraged harsher sentencing for more extended periods,
as well as more stringent practices by both police and prosecutors. Moreover,
the law has been seen as the main reason for the profound increase in mass
incarceration statistics. Not only were taxpayer dollars used to cover these new
policies, but disenfranchised communities, economically challenged families,
and individuals of color, specifically youth, were impacted.

The rate of incarcerated men of color was already on the rise when the 1994
crime bill came into place. However, the crime bill expanded penalties and
charges for juvenile offenders. Those who were most impacted were youth
from low-income communities of color. This practice is called the school-to-
prison pipeline (Shannon, 2019). The 1994 crime bill created funding for school
resource officers (SROs) who are licensed, armed police officers placed within

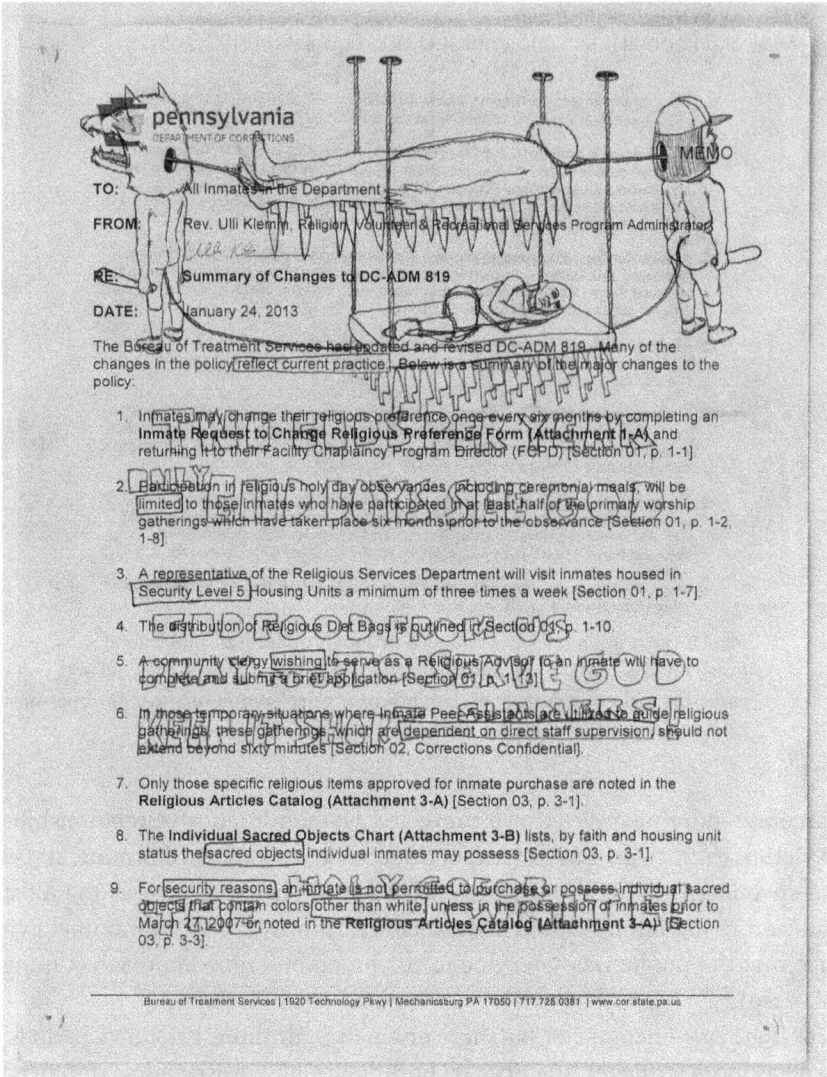

FIGURE 24   Untitled drawing on prison (from the collection of author, the artist has used prison paperwork as a backdrop to illustrate the challenging experiences of balancing incarceration and health vulnerabilities)

PAPERWORK: JAMES YAYA HOUGH

schools, and those who can make arrests. The arrest rate for Black students is twice that of their White counterparts.

According to the ACLU, Black adolescents are incarcerated five times more than White youth. Furthermore, the cost of incarcerating adolescents is $275 per day/per individual versus a community-based program that serves as an alternative to a correctional facility. Many of the charges adolescents face today are egregious responses to behaviors that previously warranted only a visit to the principal's office. One student spent twenty-one days in a juvenile detention facility for talking back in class. Another student, seven years old and living in Maryland, who shaped his pop tart into the shape of a gun, was suspended. Another group of students from North Carolina was arrested for an end-of-school-year water balloon fight. The charge? Disorderly conduct.

The statistical differences between Black and White youth are staggering. One in ten Black students have an incarcerated parent and are six times as likely to have experienced a parent behind bars at some point in their lives. Another stark difference lies in the sentencing of Black youth, who are three times as likely to be arrested for drug dealing as White youth despite being no less likely to sell drugs. Yet, the sentencing for Black adolescents is fifty percent longer than their White contemporaries (Morsy & Rothstein, 2016).

The future is dire for children who have been impacted by incarceration. Not only are they more likely to drop out, but they do worse in school and have behavioral problems. They have increased mental health issues such as anxiety and depression, as well as health problems linked to asthma and high cholesterol, which are directly linked to socio-economic strains due to living in one-parent households while the other parent is incarcerated (Morsy & Rothstein, 2016). According to Dr. Robert Kahn, incarceration expresses a failed system and a cause. The kids of incarcerated parents struggle and have been shown to have an adverse childhood experience, with an increased likelihood of being incarcerated themselves (M. D. R. Kahn, personal communication, May 23, 2023).

In addition to the severe impact of incarceration on children, it also impacts families. Having a family member incarcerated creates extreme financial stress due to the costs of bail, court fees, and fines and the costs involved in staying connected. Families are charged for phone calls, and most individuals are detained hundreds of miles, if not states away, from their homes, leaving their families with excessive travel costs for visitations. Less than one out of four people with a family member behind bars can visit their loved one during their sentence due to distance and cost (Equal Justice Initiative, December 2018).

I have witnessed firsthand the impact that incarceration can have on a child as I watched my stepmother move into the role of guardian for her grandchild when she should have been planning for retirement. Without this generational safety net, the outcome might have turned out far different. Instead, this child had a safe and loving home, a high school diploma, and a goal of graduating

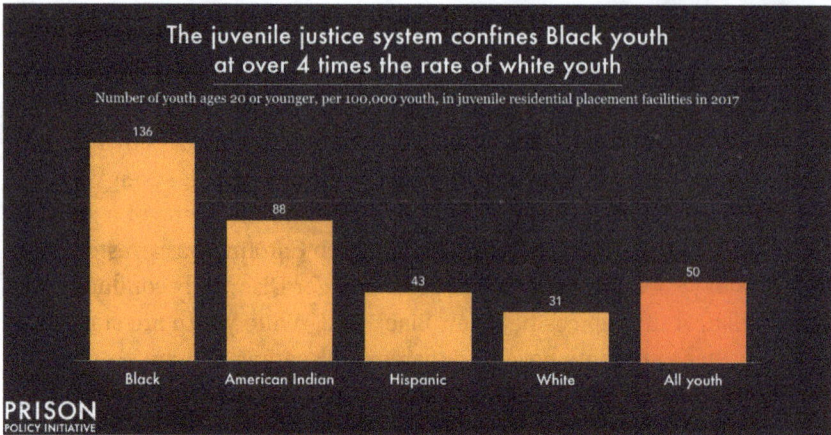

FIGURE 25   Statistics for confined black and white youth. Prison policy initiative
             GRAPH: WENDY SAWYER, 2020

from college. The stress placed on a family can be immense, leading to financial and marital strains and conflict within the family unit. Not every family can manage these additional burdens.

One person who worked as a staff nurse inside several correctional facilities for both men and women and requested anonymity discussed the need for a better support system for families, both while the individual is incarcerated and upon release. Some of the changes this former correctional nurse feels are needed include employers re-examining their hiring practices and considering jobs for ex-offenders, providing reunification counseling for families, and making it easier for families to find housing and social services to assist with mental health counseling and health care. As mentioned by this former prison employee, the United States has some of the highest rates of childhood poverty, and it is directly related to our prison system (Anonymous, February 21, 2023).

More than fifty-four percent of those who are incarcerated are considered the family breadwinner, leaving two-thirds of their families unable to meet basic needs that include food, housing, and, significantly, health care. The loss of this primary earner pushes families into catastrophic financial disasters. It highlights the traumatic impact of the carceral system. Research has shown that having an incarcerated family member increases the rates of depression, hypertension, obesity, and diabetes (Equal Justice Initiative, December 2018).

Poverty and incarceration go hand in hand. Incarceration leads to more poverty, not only for the families of the incarcerated individual but also for those who are released and trying to get stabilized while attempting to re-enter society (Anonymous, February 21, 2023). The earning income of those who have been incarcerated is forty percent less than those without a criminal background (Pew Charitable Trusts, 2010). The rate of childhood poverty for those under eighteen in the United States was 16.9% in 2021, which was 4.2% above the national average (Benson). In contrast, a family's chances of experiencing poverty increase by forty percent if the father is incarcerated (DeFina & Hannon, 2009).

The costs of incarceration are not eliminated upon release. Many states require former offenders to pay restitution and fees associated with parole conditions and supervision. Families must often choose between basic needs and post-incarceration costs. Furthermore, difficulty finding a place to live or employment further exacerbates financial instabilities. Historically, individuals with an arrest record cannot obtain housing or employment, yet a movement called "Ban the Box" is working to change that.

Commencing in 2003, the Ban the Box Campaign was started by the group All of Us or None, a national civil rights group of formerly incarcerated individuals and their families, to eliminate job and housing discrimination for those who have been convicted of a crime (Ban the Box Campaign, 2021). As of 2021, 150 counties and 37 states have adopted the policy, and the federal government has followed suit for federal agencies and contractors. Furthermore, some courts are creating policies that "ban the box" and remove questions pertaining to convictions from job and housing applications (Avery & Lu, 2021). Most of these policies impact individuals who have felonies and have been

FIGURE 26   "Ban the Box" [photograph] (Courtesy of VOCAL-NY)[2]

incarcerated in prisons. Nevertheless, the impact of shorter detention periods in local jails can also have profound effects on individuals and their families.

The 1994 crime bill not only inflated prison populations but also local jail populations. Jails account for more than 658,000 people behind bars in the 2,850 jails within the United States. However, more than 10.3 million jail admissions occurred in 2019 (Dholakia, 2023). Many of these arrests are non-violent, low-level arrests, and more than seventy-five percent of those held in local jails have not been charged with a crime, yet are unable to afford bail financially and therefore are held for weeks, months, and sometimes years before facing a judge for sentencing (Dholakia, 2023). While the bail system in the United States differs from state to state, it favors the rich overall. Those who cannot post bail remain incarcerated, regardless of innocence or guilt, until their case has a trial date. This hindrance exacerbates the risk of losing employment and disrupting their family.

Many individuals unable to make bail have died behind bars as they await a trial date while managing health complications with limited resources. Moreover, many of those who were accused were innocent. In 2016 The Huffington Post conducted a months-long investigation and found that more than 800 people had died within one year inside the nation's 3,000 city and local jails. Many of the victims of this system were defendants who were legally innocent or waiting for trial for short-sentence misdemeanors, low-level or non-violent violations such as "drug possession, traffic offenses, or probation violations, which themselves may not have led to prison time" (Wing, 2016, para. 3). New York City's Rikers Island, considered the country's most notorious jail complex and the city's largest holding center, had 19 people die in 2022 while waiting for their court hearing. According to the Vera Institute of Justice, Rikers has been described as "a torture chamber" (Bryant, 2022, para. 7).

The incarcerated writer Christopher Blackwell described his experience in a *New York Times* opinion piece, revealing the horror that can take place within the small cells of local jails. Mr. Blackwell characterizes the "disproportionate number of people experiencing addiction or chronic health conditions" despite the lack of resources and treatment that jails typically have. Furthermore, the units are overcrowded with violent offenders held with those charged with lesser crimes who cannot pay their bail while waiting for a court hearing. Due to understaffing at these facilities, the most powerful and vicious detainees control the space.

The United States has approximately 1500 prisons that are operated by 50 states. In contrast, the three thousand U.S. jails are overseen by hundreds or thousands of local jurisdictions, making it difficult to have consistency, accountability, and communication about what is happening (Blackwell,

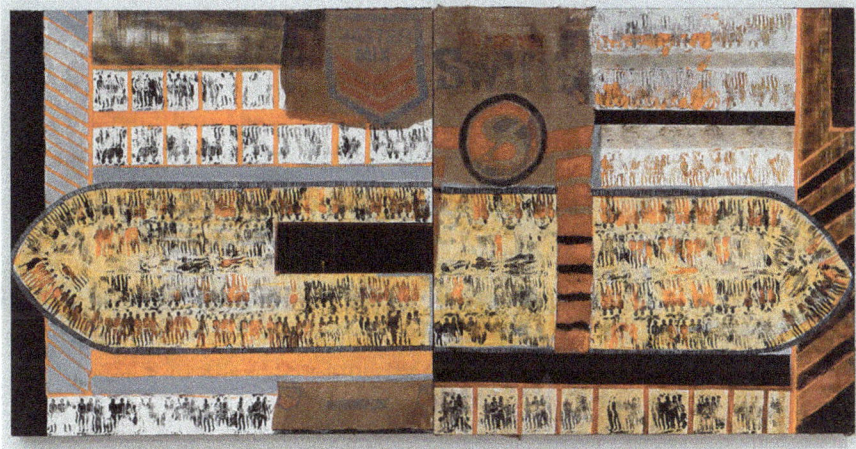

FIGURE 27   Ellapsium[3]
             DIPTYCH PAINTING: JARED OWENS

2023). One of the starkest differences between prisons and jails is suicide. The leading cause of death in jails is suicide, and the U.S. Bureau of Justice Statistics revealed that suicide rates in small jails are six times higher than the country's largest (Blackwell, 2023).

There are several reasons for this staggering difference. According to California lawyer Michael Bien, who represents several incarcerated individuals in lawsuits against the state, boredom and frustration contribute to the growing tension that exists between cellmates. The outcome of mental illness, stress, and inadequate staffing can be catastrophic and often fatal (Gabrielson & Pohl, 2019).

Inadequate healthcare in our country's correctional facilities is a leading factor in the deteriorating outcomes for those in prisons and jails. A 2014 internal investigation at New York's Rikers Island Correctional Facility reported that eighty percent of more than 100 people detained in the massive jail who sustained severe injuries from correctional officers were mentally ill (Blackwell, 2023).

The lack of consistent health care and neglect that exists within correctional facilities kills hundreds. It exacerbates existing conditions for numerous others despite the 1976 Supreme Court ruling that states, "deliberate indifference by prison personnel to a prisoner's serious illness or injury constitutes cruel and unusual punishment contravening the Eighth Amendment" (Justia, n.d.). Despite best intentions, the medical personnel who work within correctional facilities are frequently unable to assist with medical emergencies adequately. "As a nurse you are trained to care, to have a therapeutic relationship. While establishing any kind of therapeutic relationship inside the prison goes against security. And you're constantly in battle with what security wants and what adequate care is and should be" (Anonymous, February 21, 2023).

Furthermore, there are differences between women's and men's prisons, with women's facilities having up to 5 emergencies per day with issues such as seizures, heart attacks, and losing consciousness. In contrast, men's detention centers typically experience 1–2 emergencies each month, likely attributable to toxic masculinity and a reluctance to appear weak. Frequently, individuals who need to be seen will omit seeking care rather than risk losing their bunk and getting moved to a different cell with a bunkmate with whom they are unfamiliar. This decision can often lead to additional health problems (Anonymous, February 21, 2023).

The prison system in Norway stands out in stark contrast to the sobering numbers that reflect what is happening in the United States. The Scandinavian country has been making headlines for its successful prison program that produces low recidivism rates, in addition to starkly low incarceration rates of 75 per 100,000 compared to 707 for every 100,000 in the United States. These positive outcomes are attributed to their practice of restorative justice that focuses on rehabilitation rather than retribution (Sterbenz, 2014), which in turn leads to lower health complications for Norwegian prison populations. This process, in addition to the visual storytelling that formerly incarcerated artists are telling, is inspiring groups in the United States to take notice and work for change.

UCSF's Amend program is working to bring attention to this system while encouraging the United States to take notice of Norway's restorative justice model. The founder, Brie Williams, M.D., became aware of a need for change after her first day of clinic rotations as a medical student in New York. Williams asked her patient, covered with a blanket, to sit up before realizing she was handcuffed to the hospital bed. She brought this experience to UCSF and began studying the unseen health effects of imprisonment while pondering if there was a place where public health was the centerpiece of criminal justice. She found that place in Norway.

Amend was founded in 2019 with "the name a nod to the English Amendment's decree against 'cruel and unusual punishment'" (Bleicher, 2021, para. 12). Amend is seeing positive results in their work with legislators and correctional staff in seven states to shift how prisons are run. The attempt is to follow Norway's progressive leadership and focus on health and rehabilitation rather than retribution. Williams has commented, "Everyone in Norway – your taxicab drivers, your waiters – will tell you: people go to court to be punished; they go to prison to become better neighbors" (Bleicher, 2021, para. 19).

FIGURE 28   Norwegian Correctional Officers

The criminologist Bob Cameron has pinpointed five goals prisons should have: retribution, incapacitation, deterrence, restoration, and rehabilitation. Cameron believes Americans are more interested in punishment first and rehabilitation second (Sterbenz, 2014). An additional problem that plays into the punishment vs. rehabilitation stance is the lack of training for officers. A standard correctional officer training session in the United States requires only a high school diploma and a few weeks of training. However, based on Dr. Williams' experience of seeing a detained patient handcuffed to a hospital bed, an awareness of health care should be added to correctional training programs.

In contrast to U.S. programs, German officers undergo two years of college-level psychology, ethics, and communication courses. Norway officers must first complete secondary school before joining an academy for correctional service staff. This training takes two years to obtain a diploma, leading to employment as a correctional officer. One Norwegian officer remarked that they "are almost more like social workers than prison guards" (Berlioz, 2019, p. 24).

Sadly, the prospect of America catching up to these progressive European examples is a grim reality despite Williams's successes at Amend. According to the Prison Policy Initiative, state and federal prison populations decreased by

14% between January 2020 and December 2022. However, they remain danger-ous and deadly, particularly for those living with chronic illnesses. In 2018, the Department of Justice reported that state prison deaths hit the highest record in almost twenty years, with some of the deaths attributable to illness. Yet, homicides and suicides hit record-breaking numbers (The Economist, 2019).

The high rate of recidivism in the U.S., coupled with eroding facilities and warehoused detainees with limited access to family, education, consistent health care to manage chronic illnesses, and job training, is perpetuating an already dire situation. Fortunately, there are some points of hope. In addition to Amend's work, the Governor of California, Gavin Newsom, announced in early 2023 that San Quentin, one of the state's oldest prisons – also home to the country's largest death row – will get a new name and way of operating. The new focus of the San Quentin Rehabilitation Center will be on not only rehabilitation but also behavior management courses, education, job skills training, and substance abuse therapy. As Newsom commented, "This system isn't working for anybody" (Hassan, 2023).

Another example of a system shift working is in Pennsylvania. In 2018, a correctional officer team based at an institution outside of Philadelphia began researching and incorporating Scandinavian protocols into their facilities. The following year, the group traveled with researchers to Scandinavia to work alongside their Norwegian mentors. This experiment led to the prison creating a housing unit titled "Little Scandinavia," where six men, sentenced to life in prison, moved into the space.

The unit includes single cells, a communal kitchen, furnishings, and a land-scaped outdoor space. The center of the area features a large fish tank, cared for by staff and residents, encouraging people to gather and engage. Futher-more, the residents, as they are called versus the moniker of prisoners, are per-mitted to place orders with a local market for fresh foods. They go to work, treatment, or school as correctional officers engage with them. They provide a space where the residents feel safer due to positive interactions with staff and others living in the prison (Lam, 2022).

The Norway example is working. Moreover, while some U.S. justice organiza-tions are taking notice, it is a slow process to produce policy changes. However, there is hope on the horizon. The Biden-Harris Administration released a 2023 strategic plan to improve rehabilitation in jails and prisons while working to support successful reentry programs. This plan builds on the administration's Safer America Plan, which seeks to prevent and combat gun violence while cre-ating policies to improve the criminal justice system (The White House, 2023).

With awareness and improvements in new programming, there is hope that the United States can return to its 1972 statistics by implementing new programs and improved education, additional training for correctional officers and staff, eliminating revenue-generating operations and contracts, and instigating a cultural shift to support rehabilitation over punishment and improve health outcomes (Russo et al., n.d.).

Experts such as Drs. Robert Kahn and Brie Williams are doing incredible work to bring attention to the need for healthcare improvements within correctional facilities. However, several artists are working as activists, especially those who have experienced incarceration and understand the complications firsthand, presenting a visual narrative of the existing realities. Having a visual understanding of this circumstance holds the power to shift policy and perspective in ways that words sometimes cannot.

Notes

1 Mixed media on cardboard. Artwork by the author.
   Time is an elusive constraint when incarcerated. Furthermore, there is a separation of "them" and "us" concerning the guards and those who are imprisoned. The artwork represents this separation and warped sense of time, placed upon a piece of cardboard to portray the way that the United States so quickly disposes of humans through mass incarceration.
2 The "Ban the Box" movement requires employers to eliminate the question on a job application that asks about an applicant's criminal history and attempts to reduce an employers' accessibility to criminal records until later in the application process.
3 Through his mixed medium painting, Jared Owens has blurred the lines between slavery and mass incarceration. Portraying enslaved people dressed in prison orange uniforms, the artist has presented the argument that slavery has not ended but merely transformed itself into over-incarceration, especially for individuals of color. This piece incorporates soil from the prison yard where Owens served time.

References

ACLU. (n.d.) *Juvenile justice.* https://www.aclu.org/issues/juvenile-justice

Avery, B., & Lu, H. (2021, October 1). Ban the box: U.S. Cities, counties, and states adopt fair hiring policies. *National Employment Law Project.* https://www.nelp.org/publication/ban-the-box-fair-chance-hiring-state-and-local-guide/

Ban the Box Campaign. (n.d.). http://bantheboxcampaign.org

BBC. (2019, October 2018). *New York's infamous Rikers Island jail is to close.* https://www.bbc.com/news/world-us-canada-50095418

Benson, C. (2022, October 4). Poverty rate of children higher than National Rate, lower for older populations. *U.S. Census Bureau.* https://www.census.gov/library/stories/2022/10/poverty-rate-varies-by-age-groups.html

Berlioz, D. (2019). Special Report 14/36. *European Trade Union Institute.* https://www.etui.org/sites/default/files/Hesamag_19_EN-23-26.pdf

Blackwell, C. (2023, May 16). Two decades of prison did not prepare me for the horrors of county jail. *New York Times.* https://www.nytimes.com/2023/05/16/opinion/ sunday/abuse-jail-prison.html

Bleicher, A. (2021). Norway's humane approach to prisons can work here too. *UCSF Magazine.* https://magazine.ucsf.edu/norways-humane-approach-prisons-can-work-here-too

Bryant, E. (2022). [*It's*] *a torture chamber. Stories from Rikers Island.* Vera Institute of Justice. https://www.vera.org/its-a-torture-chamber

Bryant, E. (2022, May 19). *Two years of COVID-19 have fueled a crisis of isolation in prisons.* Vera Institute of Justice. https://www.vera.org/news/two-years-of-covid-19-have-fueled-a-crisis-of-isolation-in-prisons

Chung, E., Pearl, B., & Hunter, L. (2019, March 26). The 1994 Crime Bill continues to undercut justice reform—Here's how to stop it. *The Center for American Progress.* https://www.americanprogress.org/article/1994-crime-bill-continues-undercut-justice-reform-heres-stop/

Cullen, J. (2018, October 5). *Sentencing laws and how they contribute to mass incarceration.* Brennan Center for Justice. brennancenter.org/our-work/analysis-opinion/ sentencing-laws-and-how-they-contribute-mass-incarceration

DeFina, R., & Hannon, L. (2009, February 12). The impact of mass incarceration on poverty. *Journal of Crime and Delinquency, 59*(4), 562–586.

Dholakia, N. (2023, February 21). *U.S. Jails and prisons, explained. Vera.* https://www.vera.org/news/u-s-jails-and-prisons-explained

Eisen, L. B. (2020, September 1). The violence against people behind bars that we don't see. *Time.* https://time.com/5884104/prison-violence-dont-see/

Equal Justice Initiative. (2018, December 11). *Half of Americans have family members who have been incarcerated.* https://eji.org/news/half-of-americans-have-family-members-who-have-been-incarcerated/

Gabrielson, R., & Pohl, J. (2019, October 3). California tried to fix its prisons. Now County jails are more deadly. *Prison Legal News.* https://www.prisonlegalnews.org/ news/2019/oct/3/california-tried-fix-its-prisons-now-county-jails-are-more-deadly/

Ghandnoosh, N. (2021, January 22). Can we wait 60 years to cut the prison population in half? *The Marshall Project.* https://www.sentencingproject.org/policy-brief/ can-we-wait-60-years-to-cut-the-prison-population-in-half/

Hassan, A. (2023, March 25). Prisoners today, neighbors tomorrow. *New York Times.* https://www.nytimes.com/2023/03/25/us/prisons-rehabilitation-san-quentin.html

Heyboer, K., & Livio, S. K. (2020, July 2). Forced to have sex in exchange for toilet paper: Ex-inmates detail abuse by guards in N.J. women's prison. *NJ.com.* https://www.nj.com/news/2020/07/trading-sex-for-toilet-paper-and-bubble-gum-inmates-detail-abuse-by-guards-in-njs-womens-prison.html

Justia. (1976). *Estelle v. Gamble, 429 U.S. 97.* https://supreme.justia.com/cases/federal/us/429/97/

Kuhn, C. (2021, April 7). The U.S. spends billions to lock people up, but very little to help them once they're released. *PBS News Hour.* https://www.pbs.org/newshour/economy/the-u-s-spends-billions-to-lock-people-up-but-very-little-to-help-them-once-theyre-released

Lam, V. (2022, October 7). A Pennsylvania prison gets a Scandinavian-style makeover – and shows how the US penal system could become more humane. *The Conversation.* https://theconversation.com/a-pennsylvania-prison-gets-a-scandinavian-style-makeover-and-shows-how-the-us-penal-system-could-become-more-humane-187834

Morsy, L., & Rothstein, R. (2016, December 21). How does our discriminatory criminal justice system affect children? *Economic Policy Institute.* https://www.epi.org/publication/how-does-our-discriminatory-criminal-justice-system-affect-children-black-children-are-six-times-as-likely-as-white-children-to-have-a-parent-whos-been-incarcerated/

Pew Charitable Trusts. (2010, September 10). Collateral costs: Incarceration's effect on economic mobility. https://www.pewtrusts.org/en/research-and-analysis/reports/0001/01/01/collateral-costs

Russo, J., Drake, G. B., Shaffer, J. S., & Jackson, B. A. (n.d.). Envisioning an alternative future for the corrections sector within the U.S. Criminal Justice System. *Rand Corporation.* https://www.rand.org/pubs/research_reports/RR1720.html

Shannon, R. (2019, May 10). 3 Ways the 1994 Crime Bill continues to hurt communities of color. *Center for American Progress.* https://www.americanprogress.org/article/3-ways-1994-crime-bill-continues-hurt-communities-color/

Sterbenz, C. (2014, December 11). Why Norway's prison system is so successful. *Business Insider.* https://www.businessinsider.com/why-norways-prison-system-is-so-successful-2014-12

The Economist. (2022, March 19). *America's prison system is becoming more inhumane.* https://www.economist.com/united-states/2022/03/19/americas-prison-system-is-becoming-more-inhumane

The White House. (2023, April 28). *FACT SHEET: Biden-Harris administration takes action during second chance month to strengthen public safety, improve rehabilitation in jails and prisons, and support successful reentry.* https://www.whitehouse.gov/briefing-room/statements-releases/2023/04/28/fact-sheet-biden-harris-administration-takes-action-during-second-chance-month-to-strengthen-public-safety-improve-rehabilitation-in-jails-and-prisons-and-support-successful-reentry/

Widra, E. (2020, December 21). Since you asked: Just how overcrowded were prisons before the pandemic, and at this time of social distancing, how overcrowded are they now? *Prison Policy Initiative.* https://www.prisonpolicy.org/blog/2020/12/21/overcrowding/

Wing, N. (2016, July 14). Our bail system is leaving innocent people to die in jail
    because they're poor. *Huffington Post*. https://www.huffpost.com/entry/cash-bail-
    jail-deaths_n_57851f50e4b0e05f052381cb

World Population Review. (n.d.). *Recidivism rates by state*.
    https://worldpopulationreview.com/state-rankings/recidivism-rates-by-state

Installation Art

Creativity takes courage.
HENRY MATISSE

∴

Have you ever walked through a space that changed you? Emotionally or mentally? Environments that changed your perspective or made you question what you thought you knew? Or perhaps the experience provided a sense of peace or entertainment. Walking through nature provides this sense of engagement for some, whereas museums and public art present it for others. For me, walking through an art gallery or a museum space brings forth a sense of calm, provokes thought, and encourages action – a visual guide to understanding the art on the wall and myself. My engagement and observation with an exhibit contribute to the dialogue the artist conveys.

An underlying power exists when space is used to recreate and present information to a viewer. Finding new ways to slow down and take in information is invaluable in a world connected by technology and images. By creating an environment to educate, inform, and create awareness, both art installations and informative exhibitions allow an audience to absorb the images and spend time thinking about the subject matter.

Before my enlightening visit to The Legacy Museum in Alabama, an art installation at The National Underground Railroad Freedom Center in Cincinnati, Ohio, planted the seed that grew into my interest in the overlap between art and activism. The permanent exhibit titled "Invisible: Slavery Today" features, through installations, the varied ways that slavery still exists in our country. The curated show reflects how children and adults are currently exploited by displaying items such as bed frames, mannequins, mops, and everyday household items transformed into sculptural works of art. Standing before these innovatively constructed assemblages, I understood my future would entail using art as an avenue to educate and inform, particularly regarding the additional bondage endured by incarcerated individuals challenged by chronic health issues like diabetes.

© TAMARA WHITE, 2025 | DOI:10.1163/9789004710610_006

FIGURE 29   Child sex trafficking assemblage from the *Invisible: Slavery Today* exhibit at the
National Underground Railroad Freedom Center
PHOTOGRAPH: WHITE, 2017

The exact history of installation art is debatable. Still, it can be traced as far
back as 1917 when Marcel Duchamp purchased an ordinary urinal, signed it as
"R. Mutt," a pun referring to the Mott toilet manufacturers, titled the piece *Fountain*, and proceeded to enter it into the Society of Independent Artists exhibition (Mann, 2017). The artist used this controversial piece to push boundaries
and create dialogue about "deeply entrenched ideas about art" (Lesso, 2022).
Along with fellow Dadaist artists, Duchamp presented new questions and perspectives by creating artwork that used found objects and multiples in contrast
with the tradition of creating original works of art. This practice opened space
for many artists who followed (Lesso, 2022).

The term *installation* stems from the verb *to install*. However, installation
art encapsulates artwork installation and site-specific content, placement,
and creation (Suderburg, 2000). To install is a practice that happens time and
again at the beginning of each exhibition. In contrast, an *installation* is a "form

that takes note of the perimeters of that space and reconfigures it" (Suderburg, 2000, p. 4). Traditional and non-traditional mediums define installation art: painting, sculpture, found objects, drawing, text, and manufactured items. An alternative term for installation art is environments. Environments include assemblages created for a specific location and as a temporary exhibit (Tate, Installation Art, n.d.).

The history of installation art emerged from environmental art when artists turned personal, three-dimensional spaces into artistic experiences. Besides DuChamp, Allan Kaprow is considered one of the first installation artists based on his work, *Yard,* which was created in 1961. Using the space behind the Martha Jackson Gallery in New York City, Kaprow filled the backyard with black rubber car tires. Visitors were invited to interact with the environment like a giant playground. Kaprow said that art becomes closer to life when viewers participate (*Art in Context* n.d.). Kaprow would describe his first environment as a mixed media orchestra: "When you opened the door you found yourself in the midst of an entire environment... The materials were varied: sheets of plastic, crumpled up cellophane, tangles of Scotch tape, sections of slashed and daubed enamel, and pieces of coloured cloth" (Tate, Installation Art, n.d.).

Kaprow started the installation art movement in the 60s, including artists such as Marcel Broodthaers and Andy Warhol, who turned spaces into interactive installations, opening up a new market for contemporary art. The Belgian poet, artist, and filmmaker Broodthaers, who was instrumental in the early installation art scene, was known for his "highly literate and often witty approach to creating art" (Martinique, 2016, para. 1). By creating installations using unconventional items, the multi-disciplinary talent became known as a leader in the field.

One of Broodthaer's more prolific installations served as both a film set and a found-object-based art installation. *Décor: A Conquest,* a two-room experience, would be the artist's last presentation before he died in 1976. The exhibit explored the relationship between conflict and comfort. The artist's illustration of the dynamic of these two extremes, conflict, and comfort, portrays the juxtaposition between the realities faced by incarcerated individuals, particularly those managing chronic health issues. This exhibit illustrates how visual art has the power to communicate complicated topics and evoke visceral responses for viewers.

In each room, titled XIXth Century and XXth Century, the spaces embodied assemblages of war and furniture while examining the relationship between weapons and how they serve as objects of power. Furthermore, Broodthaer named the exhibit *Decor* a double entendre – with decor meaning "film set" in French, while also alluding to the interiority of interior decorating (*Art*

Monthly, 2014). This duality of space and art resembles what Andy Warhol did in his historic loft, "The Factory."

Warhol's studio space, named "The Factory" by the eccentric artist, was located in four different New York locations between 1963 and 1987 and became a famous and well-documented space where artists, celebrities, and musicians gathered. It was in these spaces that Warhol's installations, films, and silkscreens were manufactured – frequently by workers under his direction (Watson, 2003). The Factory was created during a time when artists were questioning historic practices while experimenting with not only materials but also industrial rhetoric. This new way of making art symbolized a new way of coming together, collaborating, and using the space to mimic business-like practices of assembly-line production (Jones, 2008).

Another installation artist who created an atmosphere within a site-specific space was Judy Chicago. As a University of California student in the 1960s, Chicago challenged her European history professor by pointing out the void of women discussed in the course. She would go on to create the feminist art program at California State University in 1969 (Sayej, 2017). The outspoken artist would later create *The Dinner Party*, a seminal feminist art installation that she worked on alongside 129 other artists and volunteers from 1974–1979, costing upward of $250,000 to create. The installation features plate settings for 39 leaders in women's history, including notable figures such as Georgia O'Keefe, Sacajawea, Artemisia Gentileschi, and the Primordial Goddess. Since its first showing in 1979 at The San Francisco Museum of Modern Art, the triangular banquet table has traveled to numerous museums on three continents with an audience of more than 15 million viewers (Sayej, 2017).

By the 1980s, as the art market crashed, conceptual art had a new audience and has since remained relevant. Artists such as Marcel Duchamp and the Dada movement bridged the specifics of installation art, such as using a mixture of unconventional mediums, to make way for what is now called "installative" (Bahtsetzis, 2005). Installation art burgeoned into the scene and the roots of the art form took hold. According to artist Ann Hamilton, "[a]n installation surrounds you, absorbs you into it. You are part of it the minute you step into it" (Godfrey, n.d.). Installation artists in the 80s began to have a "heightened sense of place" (Godfrey, n.d.).

In his 1988 book *Understanding Installation Art: From Duchamp to Holzer*, curator and author Mark Rosenthal discussed how the character of installation art had not yet been fully realized. Artists were creating environments in which the space had yet to be recognized as central to the understanding of the work. Rosenthal's book points to installation art becoming the predominant threat to the artwork as it emerged as a critical aspect of contemporary art.

Installation art, however, is separate from an installation of art. This ambiguity began to shift in the 80s, after years of the term being used within the art world "to describe the way in which an exhibition was arranged" (Bishop, 2005, p. 6). However, the difference lies in the viewer and the space. The audience is invited into the experience, its presence becoming a part of the installation. The presence of the viewer is the primary characteristic of the medium. Without it, space analysis becomes difficult (Bishop, 2005).

The book *Installation Art: A Critical History* examines the various modes in which an individual experiences installation art and how those assemblages create four distinct environments for the audience, including the dream scene, heightened perception, mimetic engulfment, and activated spectatorship. The Legacy Museum in Montgomery exemplifies these areas by creating an environment that engages visitors about incarceration through different modalities using video, sound, audience participation, and visual imagery.

Joining these spaces with the participants creates an organic interaction based on each interpretation. Despite variations in defining the art form and contested philosophies on the experience that installation art provides, there is a consistent agreement on the fundamental importance of the "human being who constitutes the subject of that experience" (Bishop, 2005, p. 8). The participants' experience is integral to the work.

The dream scene stems from the work by Sigmund Freud and the three characteristics of his interpretation of dreams. The first characteristic is that dreams are primarily visual, including auditory elements and sensory vividness. The second is that the dream must be broken down into components; otherwise, it will be misconstrued as a whole. Furthermore, dreams are not meant to be decoded but analyzed through free association, individual connections, and associated words (Bishop, 2005). Installations that follow the dream scene framework present surrealistic spaces that elicit unconscious connections.

Installations that follow the heightened perception theory create a space that includes a sensory overload for its viewer. By producing work that includes bright flashing lights and pulsating sounds, the work is intended to disorient and generate a hallucinatory experience. The heightened perception spaces are frequently minimalistic, allowing the elements to fill the void of material objects. Light and space are often the main features. Live installations, also called performance art, can contribute to installations within this mode. The artist Dan Graham describes these experiences as a chiasm, "a crossing over between ourselves and the world" (Bishop, 2005, p. 72).

Mimetic engulfment creates spaces that are opposites of minimalistic and post-minimalistic environments. "The possibility of locating ourselves in relation to the space is diminished, because this space is obscured, confused, or in some way intangible" (Bishop, 2005, p. 82). Installations within mimetic engulfment spaces have no sense of placement or boundaries. Each experience is intended to create a sense of altered states as the viewer attempts to find their sense of place and self within a lightless room, as darkness, mirror displacements, and video and technological fragmentations transform the experience.

The Infinity Mirror Room by Yayoi Kusama exemplifies a mimetic engulfment space. Since her initial breakthrough in experimenting with mirrors, the artist has created more than twenty of these dark, reflective spaces. Using mirrors, Kusama presents a perceptual experience for its audience, with viewers only allowed to enter the space, one party at a time. The kaleidoscopic environment presents a feeling of illusion and infinite space void of sound, leaving the visitor to reflect on oneself as reflected through mirrors and lights.

In addition to the previously mentioned environments, there is activated spectatorship. These installations are focused on decentering the audience and creating a "transitive relationship [that] is implied between activated spectatorship and active engagement in the wider social and political arena" (Bishop,

FIGURE 30   The infinity mirror room at The Broad Museum, Los Angeles, CA (an example of activated spectatorship, provides space, stillness, and reflection – physically and metaphorically – for introspection and consideration)
PHOTOGRAPH: WHITE, 2016

2005, p. 102). Some examples of activated spectatorship are exemplified through social sculptures, group materials, political art, and relational aesthetics, each having its focus yet connected through the audience's engagement.

In 1967, the artist Joseph Beuys developed the "social sculpture" theory, which states that creativity, through everyday actions and objects, could reshape society. His belief was based on the idea that life was a social sculpture that everyone helped to shape, in addition to the idea that life was art. We are all artists contributing to the design. Beuys efforts were embedded with a political stance, such as installing 7000 *Oaks*. Started in 1982 in Kassel, Germany, the artist had a goal to pair each newly planted oak tree with a four-foot-high basalt stone column installed above ground. The project took five years, with the last tree planted in 1987 (Dia Art, n.d.). Other artists have since succeeded Beuys' practice, such as Pedro Reyes, who collected weapons from residents in Cuiliacán, Mexico, in exchange for electronics. Following Beuys footsteps, the artist melted down the weapons, made shovels from the metal, and planted 1,527 trees (Tate, Social Sculpture, n.d.).

Additional processes that fall under the activated spectatorship theme include group materials encompassing community galleries and the activities within those spaces. From 1979 to 1996, one New York-based collective, Group Material, focused on just that. Creating an environment that worked drew inspiration and practice as a collective vs. individually. The motivation of the collective was to work together "against 'careerism' and reconnecting art's production and reception" (Green, 2011, para. 3) while practicing curatorial flexibility and ownership void of commercialism.

Political art is another focus under the installation art, activated spectatorship umbrella. Artists increasingly use imagery to define their beliefs and seek to inform and educate. Artists like Appleton create street art to raise awareness about type 1 diabetes. Alternatively, Jesse Krimes tells his story of using art to survive the trauma of incarceration and solitary confinement. The history of protest art is vast, and it is difficult to determine who began it and when. From Picasso's *Guernica* to the Dada movement, photographs by Gordan Parks, and the political posters of the Guerilla Girls of today, each art movement is separate yet united by a common thread of activism. Furthermore, political art falls far outside installation art and can include performances, exhibitions, billboards, and various mediums. A few prolific artists creating political art include Ai Weiwei, JR, and the group of feminist female artists, the Guerilla Girls.

With a history of political art and vocalization against the Chinese government and social injustices, Ai Weiwei has been a seminal figure in political art since the late 1990s. One of his most renowned works is *Sunflower Seeds*, created in 2010. The artist hired 1600 Chinese artisans to assist in crafting over 100

FIGURE 31
Political art in response to the
Catholic Church sex scandal.
PHOTOGRAPH: WHITE, 2021

million hand-painted, porcelain miniature sculptures that mimic the actual
seeds. The individual units were gathered and spread across the Tate Museum
gallery floor, the first exhibit of the artist's massive endeavor. Visitors were

invited to walk on and examine the seeds, created to represent the simplicity of connection amongst friends in China. Weiwei chose this typical snack to reflect personal associations from the Cultural Revolution from 1966–76, when people were stripped of their freedom, Chairman Mao was depicted as the sun to which masses of people looked up, just as one would turn upward toward a sunflower (Etherington, 2010).

Tate's Chief Curator, Sheena Wagstaff, stated, "Ai provokes a multitude of ideas, from the way we perceive number and value, to the way we engage with society at large" (Etherington, 2010). The artist encouraged viewers to walk on the work and to ask pertinent questions about our place in the world and what it means to be an individual within society. Is there power in togetherness or insignificant alone?

The photographer and elusive street artist JR presents us with similar questions. He claims to have the world's largest art museum, as he chooses to collage his work on the walls of the world, attracting an audience who would typically not go to a museum. The photographer has focused on various political themes, including women's rights, peace, and equality while presenting a core belief in humanity across global lines. One project the artist created, yet states that it was not in direct response to Donald Trump's rhetoric about building a wall along the Mexican border, inspired his curiosity about what those on the other side must be thinking. He scouted several locations until he determined that the area of Tecate was closest to the wall. There, he erected a large-scale image of a local boy, close to seventy feet high, peering over the wall with a welcoming, curious expression. The mother of the boy portrayed in the installation said that she hopes "in that image, they won't only see my kid. They will see us all" (Schwartz, 2017).

Being seen is the focus of another group with an emphasis on political art. The Guerilla Girls is a self-described anonymous artist-activist group that uses "disruptive headlines, outrageous visuals, and killer statistics to expose gender and ethnic bias and corruption in art, film, politics, and pop culture" (Guerilla Girls, n.d.). Their mission is based on the expectation of human rights for all, as they work to undermine the normative belief system while shedding light on the overlooked and unfair injustices that occur in the world. Their motto is "Do one thing. If it works, do another. If it doesn't, do another anyway. Keep chipping away!" (Guerilla Girls, n.d.).

The term relational aesthetics was coined by the art critic, historian, and curator Nicolas Bourriaud in 1998 in his book of the same name. Bourriaud described the method as "a set of artistic practices which take as their theoretical and practical point of departure the whole of human relations and their

FIGURE 32   Guerilla Girls billboard (Why does the US have 5% of the world's population but
             20% of its prisoners? 2022, © Guerrilla Girls, courtesy guerrillagirls.com)

social context, rather than an independent and private space" (Bourriaud, 1998, p. 113). Bourriaud's concept was that there was an interplay between artists and viewers, with artists serving as facilitators rather than makers.

Whether a permanent installation, an interactive event, or a non-tangible exchange between two individuals, installation art provides visitors and viewers with an experience separate from fine art hung upon a wall. Both permanent and temporary, installation art involves a mixture of materials and technologies that include video, sound, virtual reality, and interactive social media platforms. The two essential qualities that exist with all installations are space and the audience.

> The beauty of installation art lies in its vast range of different materials, mediums, and environments used to create a notion-challenging artwork. The unique concept of weaving the art piece around the viewer, and for the viewer, make it an event worth engaging in. (Lansroth, 2016)

Through the use of environments and installations, the story told through art can enhance how we receive and share information and bring forth attention to topics that often get overlooked, such as incarceration and healthcare, while encouraging shifts in the narrative in a non-threatening, creative, and thought-provoking manner. The Equal Justice Initiative has been exemplary with their Legacy Museum and National Memorial for Peace and Justice, through visuals and data-rich exhibits, by providing a connection between the racially unequal past and the current state of our justice system. They have led installation art to its full potential to educate and inform while providing a provocative art experience.

Technological advances have steeped our world in images, not only for commercial purposes. Instagram, TikTok, and ChapGPT Image Generators are becoming a standard way of communicating news and current events. These advances impact how audiences interact with images and installation environments and the rate at which they absorb the information. The filmmaker Sarah Ullman points out, "We live in such a visual world, and that's how people are used to consuming information and receiving stories" (Clipson, n.d.). Historically, art has been used as a form of activist art, and moving forward, that practice will continue to expand through installations, online formats, and as a tool for change.

FIGURE 33   Enslaved African men and women in a sculpture by the Ghanaian artist Kwame
             Akoto-Bamfo [sculpture] (The National Memorial for Peace and Justice)
             PHOTOGRAPH: WHITE, 2019

References

Art in Context. (n.d). *Installation art – Explore the different uses of installation in art.* https://artincontext.org/installation-art/

Art Monthly. (2014, February 1). Marcel Broodthaers – Décor: A conquest and bricks: 1966–1975. *Art Monthly. Reviews.*

Bahtsetzis, S. (2005, January 2). *History of installation art. Situational experience in modern art.* Personal blog.

Bishop, C. (2005). *Installation art. A critical history.* Tate Publishing.

Bourriaud, N. (1998). *Relational aesthetics.* Les Presse Du Reel Publishing.

Clipson, E. (n.d.). "*4 Creative directors tell us why the future of visual content is broader than you think.* EyeEm Blog. https://www.eyeem.com/blog/4-creative-directors-tell-us-why-the-future-of-visual-content-is-broader-than-you-think

Dia Art. (n.d.). *Joseph Beuys: 7000 Oaks.* https://www.diaart.org/visit/visit-our-locations-sites/joseph-beuys-7000-oaks

Etherington, R. (2010, October 11). Sunflower seeds 2010 by Ai Weiwei. *Dezeen.* https://www.dezeen.com/2010/10/11/sunflower-seeds-2010-by-ai-weiwei/

Godfrey, T. (n.d.). An art of the room: The haunting installations of the 1980s. *The MIT Press Reader.* https://thereader.mitpress.mit.edu/haunting-installations-of-the-1980s/

Green, A. (2011, February 1). Citizen artists: Group material. *Afterall.* https://www.afterall.org/article/citizen-artists-group-material

Guerilla Girls. (n.d.). *Guerrilla girls: Reinventing the 'F' word: Feminism.* https://www.guerrillagirls.com/about

Jones, C. A. (2008, September 26). Andy Warhol's 'factory': The production site, its context, and its impact on the work of art. *Science in Context.*

Lansroth, B. (2016, October 19). What is installation art and how does it transform our perception? *Widewalls.* https://www.widewalls.ch/magazine/installation-art

Lesso, R. (2022, June 13). What was so great about Marcel DuChamp's fountain? https://www.thecollector.com/what-was-great-about-marcel-duchamp-fountain/

Mann, J. (2017, May 9). How DuChamp's urinal changed art forever. *Artsy.* https://www.artsy.net/article/artsy-editorial-duchamps-urinal-changed-art-forever

Martinique, E. (2016, October 15). Marcel Broodthaers – The father of installation art. *Widewalls.* https://www.widewalls.ch/magazine/marcel-broodthaers

Rosenthal, M. (1988). *Understanding installation art. From Duchamp to Holzer.* Prestel Verlag.

Sayej, N. (2017, October 20). Judy Chicago: In the 1960s, I was the only visible artist. *The Guardian.* https://www.theguardian.com/artanddesign/2017/oct/20/judy-chicago-the-dinner-party-history-in-the-making

Schwartz, A. (2017, September 11). The artist JR lifts a Mexican child over the border wall. *The New Yorker.* https://www.newyorker.com/news/as-told-to/the-artist-jr-lifts-a-mexican-child-over-the-border-wall

Suderburg, E. (2000). *Space, site, intervention: Situating installation art.* University of Minnesota Press.

Tate. (n.d.). *Installation art.* https://www.tate.org.uk/art/art-terms/i/installation-art

Tate. (n.d.). *Social sculpture.* https://www.tate.org.uk/art/art-terms/s/social-sculpture

Watson, S. (2003). *Factory made: Warhol and the sixties.* Pantheon Books.

CHAPTER 6

Arts-Based Inquiry and Social Practice Art

Art is a nation's most precious heritage. For it is in our works of art that we reveal to ourselves and to others the inner vision which guides us as a nation. And where there is no vision, the people perish.

LYNDON B. JOHNSON

∴

Throughout history, "art has been used as an accessible tool for communication, raising awareness about social issues and affecting positive change" (PBS Learning Media, *Art and Social Justice*, n.d.). An arts-based inquiry approach to social justice can be expressed in multiple forms, a collaboration between art and activism and through art as a social practice. These methods serve to engage an audience. As a social-practice artist and professor, Stephanie Syjuco points out, "the best social practice projects try to attract people to join a conversation" (PBS Learning Media, *Art and Social Justice*, n.d.). Syjuco suggests that asking more questions than providing answers benefits artistic and social practices, stating that "sometimes it is about uncovering difficult truths" (PBS Learning Media, *Art and Social Justice*, 00:04:15–00:04:19, n.d.).

This social practice of art as activism led to the topic of my dissertation and, by extension, this book. It was while standing in the middle of the Legacy Museum, submerged in the experience of an interactive art exhibit focused on mass incarceration, that I questioned how people manage diabetes while they are incarcerated. The effectiveness and power of the exhibit revealed a perspective and consideration that I might not have come up with if not for the strength of the images, displays, and audio tracks that played above the space.

So, how do you use art to get people to care about social justice issues? "If it is in a museum or art gallery, people seem to understand, well, that is where art belongs. Nevertheless, when it goes out into the world and is sometimes indistinguishable from other things that happen, I think that can be beautiful" and, hopefully, enlightening (PBS Learning Media, *Art and Social Justice*, 00:02:33–00:02:44, n.d.). Bryan Stevenson created the Legacy Museum to showcase how slavery has not ended but instead has morphed into mass incarceration, which has profoundly affected how I understand contemporary mass incarceration. This message goes beyond the gallery walls and gives its audience something to consider once they exit the exhibit.

Art and advocacy have symbolically existed since time immemorial. W.E.B. DuBois once stated, "Begin with art, because art tries to take us outside ourselves. It is a matter of trying to create an atmosphere and context so that that conversation can flow back and forth, and we can be influenced by each other" (Dechow, 2015). A conversation occurs between the artist and the audience through images and a non-verbal relationship. Each participant contributes something to the story as the context gets unpacked and is grounded in perspective and individual experiences.

The focus of art as a subject and arts-based inquiry as a research method is dynamic, with new forms, theories, and philosophies contributing to the field. Understanding contemporary art and the artistic processes supports social activism as a means of participation and exploration. This practice is especially true for those incarcerated who use art as a visual narrative to translate the experience of being detained. Using these protocols is a core aspect of art and activism as creators seek to highlight social justice themes, elicit a shift in perspectives, and inspire policy changes through awareness and education. The researchers Gregory Sholette and Chloe Bass define social practice as a process that is not used merely for the sake of making art but creating work that represents instances of sociopolitical injustice (consider Picasso's Guernica), but to employ the varied forms offered by the expanded field of contemporary art as a collaborative, collective, and participatory social method for bringing about real-world instance of progressive justice, community building, and transformation (Sholette & Bass, 2018, p. XIII).

It has been suggested that artists who aim to create equity and awareness of social justice "intersect with the theories, epistemologies, and methodologies found in critical arts-based research" (Sanders-Bustle, 2020). Despite social practice frequently being overlooked and challenged as an academically revered method, many artists are interested in creating work that "focuses on the making of social change, not the making of an object" (Sanders-Bustle, 2020). Through creation, participation, and practice, action-based art is related to real-world issues such as incarceration and healthcare management and can potentially effect positive change.

For any artist, there is a vulnerability in sharing work. When the work is personal, that level of exposure increases. For the artist Kathryn DeMarco, who is living with diabetes, the art of collage provides her with a venue for self-expression while leaving room for hidden, private nuances. "What is fun for me in a collage is that I can hide stuff in there. Furthermore, that is what started

FIGURE 34 My pancrease came in a box (DeMarco, who lives with type 1 diabetes, shows the reality of living with a chronic illness and needing medical devices to stay alive.)
ARTWORK: KATHRYN DEMARCO

me with the diabetes artwork. I can hide funny stuff, sad stuff, whatever. It is like a joke to myself. Sometimes, audiences get it; sometimes, they do not. Most of the time, the hidden stuff is just something out there for people to jump to their conclusions about" (Kokernak, 2011).

Another artist creating conversation through contemporary art that focuses on diabetes is Appleton. "After surviving a diabetic coma at the age of six, Appleton began to collect almost every insulin bottle that has gone through his

FIGURE 35   Street art
            ARTWORK: APPLETON

system, amounting to hundreds of bottles, faded syringes, and old blood [test] strips" (Appleton Artwork, n.d.). The goal for Appleton is to educate and inform "the unknowing" while inspiring "the millions who have diabetes – to carry on and realize that you are not alone in this daily battle" (Appleton Artwork, n.d.). The intention of the artist pasting his work to the walls and structures in high-profile cities is to provide a connection with and for other diabetics who walk past his art. "When other people with diabetes see my work, I imagine they feel a sense of hope, community, and encouragement- to be positive and of course – that we are not alone" (qtd. in Snouffer, 2018, para. 11).

Historically, a critical thread connects artists and ailments. The desire to bring awareness and tell the story of chronic health conditions has surfaced for years. The artist Francis Goya, who died in 1828, struggled with mental health issues after becoming deaf due to an undiagnosed illness. The artist experienced hallucinations, confusion, and partial paralysis before later creating paintings such as *Yard with Lunatics,* 1793–94, that "helped him occupy his 'imagination, mortified in consideration of my ills'" (Graf, 2021).

Vincent Van Gogh was another artist who struggled with mental health issues. His famous artwork, *Wheatfield with Crows,* 1890, was one of the last paintings created by the prolific artist a short time after being released from the Saint-Paul-de-Mausole asylum, an experience much like incarceration and just months before dying by suicide. Researchers have concluded that Van Gogh likely had bipolar and borderline personality disorders and that he drank alcohol excessively. Van Gogh's most notorious breakdown occurred in December 1888, before his stay in the asylum, when the artist cut off part of his ear.

The portrayal of the wheatfields presents a solitary life under stormy skies, a road leading to nowhere, as crows hover overhead. The artist wanted the darkened sky to express both sadness and loneliness while, at the same time, presenting a healthy and fortifying countryside. Van Gogh thought of himself as similar to a bird in a cage, commenting that there

> comes a time when migratory birds fly away. A fit of melancholy – he has got everything he needs, say the children who look after him – but the sky is brooding and stormy, and deep within, he is rebelling against his misfortune. (vincentvangogh.org, n.d.)

Similarly, in the 20th century, many other individuals used art to tell the story of their medical journeys. Frida Kahlo painted many self-portraits to reveal her painful experience after a bus accident in 1925, which changed the trajectory of her life. Kahlo, confined to a bed for months, used painting to demonstrate her isolation and resilience. These artists and paintings have become recognizable today because of their health issues and use of art as a visual narrative.

Art provides an alternative to presenting information that is difficult to relate to and frequently requires empathy. Understanding how to approach art offers space to sit with each piece and interpret the image from our experiential

FIGURE 36   Wheatfield with crows (Van Gogh Museum)
ARTWORK: VINCENT VAN GOGH

history. Art lecturer and writer Kit Messham-Muir suggests three steps when observing art: look, see, and think.

1.   Look. Spend time looking at the work. The estimated time that a museum visitor stands in front of an art piece is two seconds. Look at the surface, take in the medium, and consider what the artist added or did not add to the creation.

2.   See. Some might consider seeing and looking alike; however, Messham-Muir aptly defines the difference. "Looking is about literally describing what is in front of you while seeing is about applying meaning to it." Is there iconography to be considered? Are there symbols, words, and images that have meaning behind their literal interpretation?

3.   Think. This is where the analysis comes forth. Context is important. Who is the artist? Where did the artist live? Is there a theme or subject that the artist was focusing on? It is possible that you may not know the artist, and at that moment, your context might shift the meaning of the piece. Where was I born? Who am I, and how do I look at this information? How does this work of art provoke a response from me?

When examining art, an audience has the opportunity to ponder new perspectives. Slowing down to actually *see* what's represented and working to understand the meaning behind particular images and what the artist is expressing generates a richer understanding.

Hope, empathy, and appreciation accompany the new viewpoint. Art inspires and motivates viewers, but for individuals living within a carceral system with few resources or support, art is a therapeutic method to express their experience while simultaneously communicating their realities to the outside world. While incarcerated in solitary confinement for not giving up the names of others for prosecution, Jesse Krimes created work that would eventually be exhibited in major museums across the country. James Yaya Hough used his numerous Department of Corrections forms as a backdrop for his sketches about life inside a prison. As best said by French artist Andre Maurois, "Art is an effort to create, besides the real world, a more humane world" (Phillips, n.d.).

The work within this book falls into the category of social justice art. By examining relevant and urgent social justice structures such as incarceration, the arts can "help us remember, imagine, create, and transform the practices that sustain oppression as it endures across history and locality" (Bell & Desai, 2011). Furthermore, social justice art should "awaken our senses and ability to imagine alternatives that can sustain the collective work necessary to challenge entrenched patterns" while shifting the encompassing narrative institutions entrenched with old ways of thinking (Bell & Desai, 2011). As Mark Valdez asks on his blog, ARTSblog, on the *Americans for the Arts* website, "What if we stopped thinking about art and social justice and instead looked at art as social justice?" How can we expand our meaning of social justice by including art to communicate the disparities within our communities? Instead of separating art and justice, there is value in viewing art as the channel from which we get our information.

Sometimes, not saying something has more power than too many words. As the saying goes, a picture can be worth a thousand words. Take, for example, the movements of Banksy or artist Ai Wei Wei. Both visual artists shed light on social and political injustices through installation and street art, inviting arts-based inquiry about specific topics. Arts-based inquiry and social justice are natural partners in increasing and creating social impact (Power, 2014). They are a process by which the artist manipulates material and symbolic tools for "the reconstruction of social and cultural meaning" (Power, 2014).

Using these methods and practices to examine incarceration's systemic impact on individuals and families, numerous artists are creating a shift in the narrative of the carceral system, both politically and socially. Support for many artists surfaced through the Art For Justice Fund, created by the philanthropist Agnes Gund in 2017. After selling her 1962 Roy Lichtenstein painting "*Masterpiece*" for $150 million, Gund directed the money into a five-year fund. In collaboration with the Ford Foundation and advisors from Rockefeller Philanthropy, Art For Justice would go on to provide over 400 grants to more than 200 organizations and artists working to eradicate mass incarceration.

Several individuals who received an Art For Justice grant are presenting the realities and injustices of incarceration through artistic expression and storytelling in various formats. Some work commenced inside prison walls, and a few artists continue collaborating with those who have yet to be released. The artist Jared Owens, featured in Chapter 4 and shown in Figure 36, incorporates smuggled prison yard soil into his painting to present the inhumanity of incarceration. Owens describes the intention of the work as how to "best represent what we know exists but can't always articulate" (Waddoups, 2022). The combination of the soil and paint adequately portrays the gritty and abrasive existence of living behind bars.

Another artist who was one of the first recipients of Agnes Gund's fund is Jesse Krimes. While incarcerated in Pennsylvania, Krimes covertly worked on several works of art, including items found within the prison. The prolific artist used bedsheets, magazines, hair gel, and prison soap to create a masterful collection of art on fabric. Over his five-year sentence, Krimes made 39 panels that he mailed to his girlfriend, one at a time, and later stitched together into a massive 40-foot wide quilt titled *Apokaluptein:16389067:II*. The quilt showcases

FIGURE 37   Series III #11 by Jared Owens
PHOTOGRAPH: MALIN GALLERY

the artist's experience of creating art as a survival mechanism throughout incarceration. Krimes stated that "artwork facilitated conversation. And it humanized me to some of the guards. They saw me not as an inmate but as a person" (Hohenadel, 2014).

In 2017, Krimes and the formerly incarcerated artist Russell Craig co-founded the Right of Return Fellowship, which was established to help other formerly incarcerated artists and creators support work that advances criminal and racial justice. In 2023, Jesse Krimes was named Executive Director of the newly established Center for Art and Advocacy, one of the last significant grants the Agnes Gund Art For Justice Fund provided. The mission of the center is to create "a direct path to sustainability and equity by developing a multi-purposed network dedicated to impacted artists" (Center for Art and Advocacy, n.d.) through exploration and dialogue about transformative justice, how art is critical to the community, and to support formerly incarcerated artists develop new skills and step into leadership roles and mentor others who follow.

The Art for Justice Grant and Right of Return Fellowship have inspired me to follow their lead with grant-making and create a non-profit gallery space in Cincinnati, Ohio, that will encourage curiosity, creativity, and activism through the intersectionality of art, education, and social justice. The Bader + Simon Empowerment grant will emphasize projects embedded in social justice and

FIGURE 38   Polanski by Jesse Krimes (image transfer on a prison bed sheet with graphite,
             magazine, hair gel, and prison soap, from the collection of the author)
             PHOTOGRAPH: MALIN GALLERY

support underrepresented artists by providing them 100% of sales for exhibits at the Bader + Simon Gallery, which is scheduled to open in 2025.

Jesse Krimes, Jared Owens, Russell Craig, and numerous others have found a career sharing their stories through an arts-based practice. Many have gained recognition through the ongoing exhibit *Marking Time: Art in the Age of Mass Incarceration* that followed the book by the same name, authored by Dr. Nicole R. Fleetwood, Professor of American Studies and Art History at Rutgers University and curator of the exhibit. By highlighting over thirty-five artists in the show, the exhibition examined "the work of artists within U.S. prisons and the centrality of incarceration to contemporary art and culture" (MOMA, 2020–2021). The book and the exhibit feature art by people in prison and those working to bring erasure and attention to imprisonment and mass incarceration.

Fleetwood's book was published in 2020, and the first exhibit was displayed at MOMA's PS1 space in Queens, New York, and received international acclaim. It has since traveled to numerous locations within the United States and was updated after the COVID-19 pandemic to include work that reflects the crisis that occurred within U.S. prisons, in addition to the ongoing health emergencies for incarcerated communities. The website for the exhibit notes that the work grew out of research on contemporary culture, art, and the carceral system. Dr. Fleetwood interviewed both currently and formerly incarcerated artists and reflects that "with meager supplies and in the harshest conditions, imprisoned artists find ways to resist the brutality and isolation that prisons engender" (Marking Time, n.d.).

The artist Sable Elyse Smith uses her craft to present the trauma of incarceration in her piece *The Body Keeps the Score*. Heavily hued in tones of blue, Smith uses the color to reflect on the many ways that blues are tied to incarceration. The color is associated with melancholy and depression, blues music, the pale blue walls of prison cells, and the color of prison uniforms. The title of Smith's work is based on the book of the same name by Bessel van der Kolk, which discusses the often unseen health complications of trauma and stress that manifest while incarcerated.

The self-portrait drawing by Billy Sell is another artist featured in *Marking Time*. Sell's work has been widely circulated by activists working to highlight the progression of mental health that stems from extended periods of solitary confinement. After participating in a mass hunger strike to bring attention to solitary confinement, Sell requested medical treatment and ultimately died after receiving none. The Department of Corrections deemed Sell's death a suicide after he was found strangulated and unresponsive. However, advocates have underlined the psychological deterioration that occurs in solitary cells. Billy Sell's portrait is a haunting reminder of this as his image stares directly at the viewer in an attempt to "express the totalizing impact of the immobility, penal isolation, and sensory control enforced by such restrictive states of captivity" (Fleetwood, 2020, p. 191).

FIGURE 39　The body keeps the score by Sable Elyse Smith (© Sable Elyse Smith, Courtesy Regen Projects, Los Angeles and Carlos/Ishikawa, London)

FIGURE 40   Self-portrait by Billy Sells

Dr. Fleetwood's book brought the intersection of art and incarceration into the modern-day spotlight. However, prison art as a social practice has existed for years. In 2019, The Drawing Center, located in New York City, exhibited the show *The Pencil is the Key*, featuring approximately 140 drawings by more than 50 artists. Many artists had been drawing before incarceration, and others found their craft behind bars. The catalog for the exhibit describes incarceration as "any situation in which an individual is denied their freedom" (Steinhauer, 2019). Therefore, many of the works on display covered a range of circumstances, from the French Revolution to the Soviet Gulag, mental institutions, and what is most commonly thought of when incarceration is discussed – U.S. prisons.

While the *Marking Time* exhibition examines the work of artists within U.S. prisons and a visual narrative of incarceration within contemporary art, the *Drawing Room* show has a wide breadth of work, origin, and periods of the artists and their featured work. Identities of the artists and their presumed innocence or guilt are included in the wall labels as the exhibit seeks to present "the fundamental nature of creative expression and what it means to be incarcerated" (Steinhauer, 2019). Both exhibitions, however, showcase how a socially engaged practice through art provides a medium to engage social discourse amongst viewers.

Social practice art uses temporary exchanges of human interactions to push back against societal norms by inviting a range of producers to create work, including professional artists, non-profit organizations, and social service institutions (Zanghi, 2021). Within the museum community, social practice is often synonymous with outreach and education (Davis, 2013), demonstrating how visual art can define the challenges of incarcerated individuals dealing with chronic health issues, possibly encouraging activism on their behalf.

The 1990s contemporary art world birthed social practice art by accepting the intersection of the two perspectives, art and activism, with an ethos of placing viewers at the core of the project while committing to making positive social contributions. Additionally, social practice art resists traditional objectification of art by institutions. It opposes any sense of alienation that can exist within a divided society. Instead, the art brings forth a sense of community among outsiders and interested viewers and provides an awareness of injustice.

While museums are art-centric institutions, they are also financially incentivized entities. Many art institutions, such as museums, are run like corporate companies with strict policies, budgets, and boards of directors superseding curatorial decisions. Furthermore, trends and trailblazing creatives incentivize commercial galleries that garner fifty percent of sales. With the influx of formerly incarcerated artists making the rounds in the art world, there is a potential for exploitation and opportunistic directors focusing on finances over the well-being of artists.

There is a history of museum funding coming from the ultrarich of yesterday, such as Henry Clay Frick, John D. Rockefeller, and Andrew Carnegie, to the disgraced Sachler family of today. One particular institution fell under scrutiny for investing in private, for-profit prisons. In 2019, artists, curators, and academics brought attention to the MoMA Museum in New York City, along with trustee Larry Fink, CEO of the financial firm BlackRock. The controversy stemmed from BlackRock's investments in GEO Group and CoreCivic, two companies operating private prisons. Furthermore, MoMA's affiliation with Fidelity Investments, which owns stock in private prison companies, was used to manage the art institution's pension fund (Kinsella, 2019). A signed petition, released by the group Art Space Sanctuary, was released to the press and states:

> These prisons punish for profit, break up families and communities, detain immigrant children, and impede visits. These prisons are racist and violent and routinely violate human rights. Detained Migrants are denied due process. These prisons cut costs, deny medical care, and serve barely edible food.

Today, many individuals who have sat behind the bars of institutions similar to CoreCivic prisons are now exhibiting in some of the most prestigious museums in the United States and beyond. Their work educates the public on the mass incarceration epidemic in the United States while presenting an argument for using art to provide a narrative. The protests of MoMA and Larry Fink starkly contrast the previous tendencies of artists and curators who have had to self-center opinions and cater to the wonts and interests of wealthy supporters and patrons (Lieberman, 2019).

By highlighting the discrepancies within the museum world, social practice art steeped in social justice topics by underrepresented voices can help redefine what is needed for progress in supporting artists while working toward an equitable society. Many museums have educational departments that utilize the concepts of social practice art, highlighting topics such as incarceration and injustice. The key to making a lasting change is ensuring that the administrators and board of directors are eager to support this form of art-making while adequately supporting the creators that make exhibits possible.

References

Appleton Artwork. (n.d.). Appleton art works. *Diabetes awareness through art.* https://appletonartwork.com/about/

Bell, L. A., & Desai, D. (2011). Imagining otherwise: Connecting the arts and social justice to envision and act for change: Special issue introduction. *Equity & Excellence in Education, 44*(3), Social Justice in the Arts.

Center for Art and Advocacy. (n.d.). https://centerforartandadvocacy.org/

Davis, B. (2013, July). A critique of social practice art." *International Socialist Review. 90.* https://isreview.org/issue/90/critique-social-practice-art/

Dechow, S. L. (2015, September 2). Begin with art. *The Listening.* http://welcometothelistening.org/blog/2015/8/26/begin-with-art

Graf, S. (2021, September 5). How mental illness shaped the works of these 5 artists. *The Collector.* https://www.thecollector.com/how-mental-illness-shaped-works-by-artists/

Hohenadel, K. (2014, March 19). The art of doing time. *Slate.* https://slate.com/human-interest/2014/03/philadelphia-artist-jesse-krimes-uses-a-70-month-jail-sentence-to-create-a-monumental-work-of-contraband-art-photos.html

Kinsella, E. (2019, April 29). Artists, curators, and academics call on MoMA and trustee Larry Fink to divest from private prisons. *ArtNews.* https://news.artnet.com/art-world/academics-call-moma-divest-profit-prisons-1529356

Kokernak, J. (2011, April 12). Diabetes in art: A conversation with Kathryn DeMarco. https://asweetlife.org/?p=15342

Lieberman, R. (2019, September 23). Painting over the dirty truth. *The New Republic.* https://newrepublic.com/article/154991/rich-art-museum-donors-exploit-identity-politics-launder-reputations-philanthropy

Marking Time. (n.d.). https://markingtimeart.com/

Messham-Muir, K. (2014, October 22). Three simple steps to understand art: Look, see, think. *The Conversation*. http://theconversation.com/three-simple-steps-to-understand-art-look-see-think-33020

Museum of Modern Art. (2020–2021). *Marking time. Art in the age of mass incarceration*. https://www.moma.org/calendar/exhibitions/5208

PBS. (n.d.). Art and social justice. *Learning Media*. https://www.pbslearningmedia.org/collection/art_socialjustice/

Phillips, R. (n.d.). Quotes about the benefits of art & art-making. *The Healing Power of Art & Artists*. https://www.healing-power-of-art.org/benefits-of-art/

Power, S. (2014, September 4). Arts-based inquiry: The natural partner for social justice. *Teacher Magazine*. https://www.teachermagazine.com.au/articles/arts-based-inquiry-the-natural-partner-for-social-justice

Sanders-Bustle, L. (2020). Social practice as arts-based methodology: Exploring participation, multiplicity and collective action as elements of inquiry. *Art/Research International: A Transdisciplinary Journal, 5*(1).

Sholette, G., & Bass, C. (2018). *Art as social action*. Allworth Press.

Snouffer, E. (2018, July 26). Art and diabetes: 'Appleton was here'. *Diabetes Voice*. https://diabetesvoice.org/en/diabetes-profiles/art-and-diabetes-appleton-was-here/

Steinhauer, J. (2019, December 12). Prison art, a dark place where the Muse never leaves. *New York Times*. https://www.nytimes.com/2019/12/12/arts/design/the-pencil-is-a-key-review-drawing-center.html

Thompson, N. (2015). *Seeing power: Art and activism in the 21st century*. Melville House Publishing.

Valdez, M. (2015, October 27). Art as social justice. *ArtsBlog*. https://blog.americansforthearts.org/2019/05/15/art-as-social-justice

Van Gogh, V. (n.d.). Paintings, drawings, quotes, and biography. *Wheatfield with Crows, 1890 by Vincent Van Gogh*. https://www.vincentvangogh.org/wheat-field-with-crows.jsp

Waddoups, R. (2022, November 28). With prison yard soil, Jared Owens paints the inhumanity of incarceration. *Surface*. https://www.surfacemag.com/articles/jared-owens-anthem-x-malin-gallery/

Zanghi, A. (2021, March 3). How art connects prisons and museums. *Current Affairs*. https://www.currentaffairs.org/2021/03/how-art-connects-prisons-and-museums

Conclusion

> Artwork is a very powerful tool to challenge people's perspectives against who we view in society as who is disposable and who is valuable.
>
> JESSE KRIMES

••

I never thought that Montgomery, Alabama, would change my life. Yet walking through the doors of the Legacy Museum elicited a perspective that would become the focus of research for my dissertation and this book. *What does someone do if they are incarcerated and living with diabetes?* The thought immediately hit me as I carefully traversed the exhibit filled with photographs, video displays, written letters by imprisoned children, and audio recordings playing overhead. This experience was so profound that mid-way through my visit, I had to find a bathroom to release my pent-up anger and anxiety through tears and deep breaths that were building within me.

I was startled not only by the thought of diabetes and incarceration but also by the power of the exhibit. The curatorial combination of artwork, images, and sounds provoked my dissertation topic and this book while portraying how art can create change and shift perspectives. Furthermore, it provides a space for empathy and understanding a frequently stigmatized topic. This book expands on my experience at the Legacy Museum by examining the intersection of incarceration and chronic healthcare management.

Living with a medical condition can be precarious, as is incarceration. However, living with health complications when someone else holds the very medication and supplies that can prevent a fatal outcome creates an especially powerless and vulnerable situation for thousands of individuals living behind bars, many of whom are people of color or from disenfranchised communities.

I frequently state that we are not born on an equal playing field and imagine what life might look like if that were the case. Instead, we exist within a world founded on finances and fortuitous genetics. The disparities that exist within healthcare and carceral systems are indicative of this lottery system. Communities of color account for thirty percent of the United States population, yet are incarcerated at a rate of sixty percent, far higher than their white counterparts. Furthermore, the United States spends over $180 billion to staff, track, and support the more than two million individuals behind bars.

The 1970s saw the rates of incarceration increase as past Presidents espoused the need for strict sentences, followed by California's Three Strikes Law of the 90s, which many other states have mimicked. Suddenly, individuals with a third arrest were given a lifetime penalty regardless of the offense. Further impacting the growing prison population was President Bill Clinton's Violent Crime Control and Law Enforcement Act, later called the 1994 Crime Bill, a single decision that would both complicate and confuse sentencing. The law incentivized increased incarceration rates while providing additional protection for domestic abuse cases with an assault weapons ban.

This protocol increased arrests and sentencing, which, in turn, led to more prisons and jails being erected nationwide. Despite showing evidence of improved public safety, the 1994 bill stands as the most enormous crime bill in U.S. history. This extreme decision has not made the country safer, as The United States continues to be a leader in incarceration and recidivism rates. Furthermore, the spread between White and Black adolescents is vast, with Black youth incarcerated five times more than White individuals. Black children are six times as likely to have a parent incarcerated at some point throughout their lives. These statistics significantly impact not just these adolescents' academic success but also their mental and physical health.

For those who have served their time, the punishment does not end with a prison gate exit. Securing safe housing, employment, and quality health care is arduous, especially with a felony and prison time. Life becomes a series of precarious challenges as one tries to re-enter a world that fails to see them as equal. Unlike Norwegian prisons that provide rehabilitation and security upon release, the United States never stops punishing despite completed sentences and lives being turned around. Even those later deemed innocent suffer the stigma of having been locked away. Entering a prison within the United States, for any reason, leaves a nearly impossible residue to wash out.

The after-effects of incarceration are intertwined with many other factors that fall under the definition of social determinants of health. Factors such as level of education, socio-economic status, race, gender, and the community where one lives all have an impact on a person's odds of entering the penal system and define how they will manage once released from prison. Nevertheless, we never let people off the hook in a country with the most billionaire citizens. We punish people for being poor, having too much melanin, and frequently being in the wrong place at the wrong time.

One of the most significant hurdles for people exiting a correctional facility is finding adequate health care to support newly diagnosed and pre-existing conditions. Many newly released people have admitted that their health issues surfaced behind bars due to increased stress, poor dietary options, and tightly controlled access to medical care. These pre-existing and newly acquired health complications contribute to homelessness and bankruptcy in the United States. Chronic illnesses such as diabetes pose additional difficulties for incarcerated individuals, given the urgency and fatal outcomes if someone living with the disease is not provided their medications on time. Unfortunately, with incarceration comes little to no control over access to necessary medical supplies.

As the mother of a daughter with type 1 diabetes, I am fully aware of the imperative need for immediate access to insulin and supplies. This understanding brought forth the beginnings of my research and this book. It is unfathomable to me that someone locked behind bars can adequately maintain consistent health outcomes without having some control over their medications. However, this is the reality for so many incarcerated individuals.

The COVID pandemic of 2020 heightened the lack of control that those behind bars felt. Thousands of incarcerated individuals were exposed to the virus while locked up in tight quarters without adequate supplies. By early 2023, approximately three thousand people had died from COVID-19, and another 645,000 had been infected. Numerous correctional officers refused to receive the vaccine, leaving prison populations vulnerable and substantially impacted, with little resources for masks and sanitization supplies. The pandemic also significantly interfered with family visits, leaving people behind bars exposed, vulnerable, and isolated from their support systems.

Furthermore, family support is a significant factor for incarcerated people, especially those with chronic illnesses. Having access to additional support and supplies can have a positive outcome for individuals. As reflected in the practices of Norwegian prisons, being incarcerated close to family while having access to job training, therapy, and social services has proven to reduce incarceration and recidivism rates significantly. The correctional facilities within the United States have failed to provide equal rehabilitation. However, many incarcerated people have found their therapeutic resources through art making.

Art and activism have an active role in social justice topics, intending to inform and educate, yet for incarcerated communities, art can serve as a tool to occupy time and channel the stress of prison life. Perhaps even more importantly, art is a visual narrative of one's experience. W.E.B. DuBois reminded us that art takes us outside of ourselves and elicits a conversation between the maker and the audience, influencing and informing. Art provides a venue for complex topics, to approach intense emotions, and provide another way to communicate the realities of living with chronic health concerns and incarceration.

Several artists created work while incarcerated and have since discovered a thriving career in the art world. Many of these artists are in my personal art collection and piqued my interest in the visual representation of a circumstance. Jared Owen's piece, Ellapsium v, featured in Chapter 4, is a mix-media diptych that includes prison yard soil mixed into the paint. Several other artists who have found their footing through the prolific exhibition Marking Time, curated by Nicole Fleetwood, have created visual narratives of their time behind bars. The recent interest in their work is a hopeful reflection that the awareness around prison brutality and over-incarceration is increasing.

In addition to artwork, some prisons and organizations within the United States are beginning to create a shift in antiquated practices that did little to keep communities safer or keep people from reoffending through programming changes. The AMEND program at the University of California San Francisco, founded by Brie Williams, works with wardens to improve the culture within U.S. prisons while treating incarcerated populations with care and dignity. Furthermore, William's team uses a multi-team approach to guide prisons in creating improved healthcare systems.

As a society, we must remember the imbalances that exist within our country. To pause before making judgments about a person's circumstances. The United States is one of the wealthiest countries in the world, housing the most billionaires worldwide. Yet, we have people living on the streets, frequently without assistance. We have innocent people locked up for years awaiting trial because they cannot afford bail, and our healthcare system not only bankrupts families but discriminates against those without adequate health insurance.

We are all human, and we deserve to be recognized as such. As the artist Jesse Krimes points out, we are all offenders, whether running a red light or not paying a parking ticket. Some people are born with more means than others, whether financially, having family support, or being part of a race or culture that fares better. However, it comes down to supporting those in need.

For those locked up within our prison systems, we must allow people to do their time, serve their sentences, and then permit them to re-enter society to do better. These people are valuable voices in our communities. Many of their stories are reflected through art. Artists like Russell Craig and Jesse Krimes, both featured in Marking Time and my collection, have created fellowships to help newly released people thrive and represent what is possible when you allow people to live up to their potential, exemplified by the success rates of the Norwegian Department of Corrections. There is only the possibility of change if we accept the realities of the broken penal system within the U.S. As a society, we must work to be the change that can make a difference for many families. When considering a punitive vs. rehabilitative penal system, ask yourself, who do you want as your neighbor?

As I deliver these last words and write the last sentence of a book that has been with me for years, germinating through graduate school discussions and road trip explorations, I also want to create change. Through an expanding art collection that focuses on underrepresented artists and the visual narratives that present provocative considerations, I want to be part of a society that makes change for the better using activist art.

As of this writing, the non-profit gallery Bader+Simon, located in Cincinnati, Ohio, is underway and will feature art that examines the intersection of art, education, and social justice. In addition to the annual Bader + Simon Empowerment Grant that supports an artist working on a project embedded in social justice and aligns with the organization's mission, the gallery will provide artists with 100% of the sale of their art.

In the words of Manuel Oliver, artist and founder of Change The Ref, "you do what you do best" when working to change the system. This book, this art, and the future of Bader + Simon is my effort, my best, to shed light on a rarely discussed topic that needs some understanding, perspective, and policy changes. Remember Bryan Stevenson's sentiment that we are all better than the worst thing we have done.

Artist Spotlights

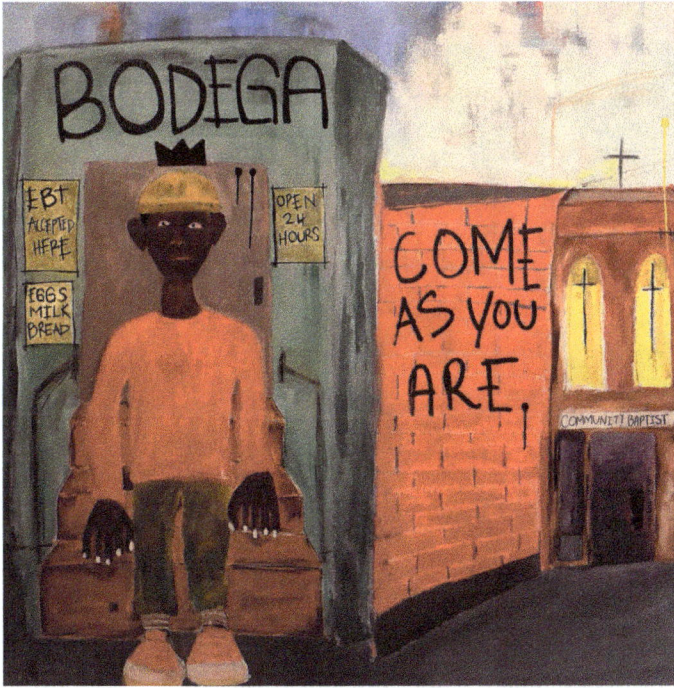

Through the lens: Bodega, 2022
PAINTING: SHANEQUA BENITEZ

Shanequa Benitez personifies the resilience inherent in adversity. Through her art, Benitez not only reflects the essence of contemporary times but also embraces it as a medium for personal storytelling, enabling her to reclaim her narrative on her own terms. Raised in the housing projects of Yonkers, NY, she confronted the harsh realities of drugs from a tender age. At the age of 18, she became entangled in the drug trade, an unfortunate turn of events that resulted in a broken jaw stemming from a botched transaction. Witnessing the loss of friends to violence or incarceration served as a profound awakening for her. In 2010, the artist's transformative journey found a pivotal moment when she was featured in the documentary "The House I Live In." This influential film shed light on America's ineffective and costly War on Drugs, as well as its dysfunctional prison system. Benitez attributes her involvement in this documentary as a catalyst that forever altered the trajectory of her life. Today, she channels her focus into artistic endeavors encompassing painting, photography, and writing. Additionally, Benitez has ventured into the realm of clothing design.

© TAMARA WHITE, 2025 | DOI:10.1163/9789004710610_009

Through the lens: Appleton photograph, Street Art NYC

Appleton is an artist and photographer who creates art, images, and sculptures. After surviving a diabetic coma at the age of six, he began to collect almost every insulin bottle that had gone through his system, amounting to hundreds of bottles, faded syringes, and old blood strips.

Before he was born, his sister Beatrice died in the 1970s at the age of seven due to unrecognized diabetes. She died of diabetic ketoacidosis (DKA) seven years before Appleton's diagnosis. Awareness was previously low, and doctors thought that Beatrice was suffering from a common cold. Despite modern-day advances, kids still die from unrecognized Type 1 Diabetes.

Today, Appleton inspires millions of people with diabetes to persevere and realize they are not alone in the daily battle. By using art, the street artist seeks to raise and spread awareness by putting his message on the streets, asking passersby to wonder what they are seeing, what they are looking at, and to consider the situation that over 30 million American people with diabetes look at every day.

Through the lens: *School to Prison* installation (Installation by Aimee Wissman, Courtesy of the artist)

PHOTOGRAPH: TONY WALSH

"When you're incarcerated, you are forced into community." That was Aimee Wissman's belief as she served a sentence at the Dayton Correctional Institute for Women (DCI) in Ohio.

As a way of coping and understanding the path that stemmed from her unstable childhood, Wissman picked up available drawing materials and started copying images from books and magazines.

She went on to explore freehand drawing before exploring painting. "The way that I like to approach painting is that I just kind of start on background work, and I build layers. Ink, acrylic, charcoal, chalk, whatever!" Her art process, while incarcerated, changed her relationship with everyday items that could be utilized to create.

Wissman is not only a painter but also a screenwriter and filmmaker of *For They Not Know*, a film that explores a woman's journey to overcome heroin addiction and is co-founder of the Returning Artists Guild that supports currently and formerly incarcerated artists.

Through the Lens: Rikers Island
Jail Cell, 2020
CURATED AND PHOTOGRAPHED: STEVEN AND WILLIAM LADD

"Jail Cell" was made in collaboration with Steven and William Ladd and those in custody at Riker's Island's George R. Vierno Center, North Infirmary Command, Otis Bantum Correctional Center, Anna M. Kross

Center, and the Manhattan Detention Complex, as well as over 500 people from our community on the outside.

"What one word describes incarceration for you?"

The words lining this installation piece are responses to that question. We engaged with over 125 people in custody in five jails and hundreds more from the outside community to build these word blocks.

In the summer of 2020, outside visitors were prohibited from entering the jail system, so we had to find a way to engage with those in custody without being in direct contact. Usually, in our Scrollathons®, each participant makes a colorful scroll to keep and another as part of a collaborative piece. When we learned that those in custody had access to colored pencils, we sent out packets that included a drawing of blank scrolls for them to color so they could still create and keep their own work of art. We explained in the packet how we use art to tell stories and encouraged them to think of their own story that inspired the coloring and left space for them to write it out and sign and date their work.

We also asked them to return anonymous responses to the prompt: "What one word describes incarceration for you?" We also added responses from the outside community, bringing inside and outside together. The result was an art installation in the form of a jail cell filled with those responses on the inside.

Sable Elyse Smith is an interdisciplinary artist, writer, and educator who creates a visual narrative about incarceration, politics, and the personal journey through multiple mediums such as video, sculpture, photography, and text. Many of Smith's artworks focus on the "carceral state primarily through its impact on the body and subjectivity" (Fleetwood), as Smith spent many days of her youth visiting her father in prison.

The sculpture shown below, which mimics a toy jack, is titled *Riot III* and made with seats from prison visiting room tables. The design of the prison tables is purposefully uncomfortable, with limited space between the tabletop and seat to inhibit people from passing things under the table. Furthermore, the structures keep a distance between those who are incarcerated and the family members visiting them. Smith's artwork reflects the intent of prison environments and the trauma that is placed among both family members, and the trauma emanates from carceral systems.

Through the Lens: *Riot III* by Sable (© Sable Elyse Smith. Courtesy Regen Projects, Los Angeles and Carlos/Ishikawa, London)

Reference

Fleetwood, N. R. (2020). *Marking time. Art in the age of mass incarceration.* Harvard University Press.

Index

www.ingramcontent.com/pod-product-compliance
Lightning Source LLC
Chambersburg PA
CBHW050535270326
41926CB00015B/3240